INTRODUCTION

Shortly after the publication of *The Bread Machine Cookbook*, which was the first cookbook available for bread machine owners, I started receiving hundreds of letters from bread machine owners. Many of the letters contained questions about bread machine baking (relating to both machines and recipes) which the manufacturers were unable to answer. (Now many manufacturers have toll-free numbers with consumer service departments or home economists, but that was not the case just a few years ago.) Many letters were from people who were having so much fun with their machines that they simply wanted to correspond with other bread machine owners to share hints and tricks which they had discovered, and recipes which they had adapted or developed.

Fate, it seemed, was pushing me into what has become *The Bread Machine Newsletter*. This newsletter has become a participating forum for bread machine owners to share their hints, ideas, stories and recipes and a place to get answers to their bread machine baking questions, whether easy or difficult. Many of the hints and ideas in the pages that follow were sent to me by excited bread machine owners who have used my books and/or newsletter subscribers. I hope you enjoy them as much as I.

The recipes in this book were developed by or adapted at the request of other people. Some are recipes which have been handed down from generation to generation and have now been adapted to bread machine size and use. Others are new recipes which people have developed. Once a recipe was sent to me, I tested it in the machine for which it was developed. My team of testers and I then tested it in other machines to ensure that it works successfully. It was sometimes necessary to make slight changes to the recipes submitted so that the recipe will work in all machines. I have made every effort to keep the original flavor, texture and theme of each recipe submitted.

BREAD MACHINE BASICS AND HINTS

If you have just received a bread machine and you are not sure how to use it, I strongly recommend reading two things:

1. The owner's manual which came with the machine.
2. The introductory chapters of this book which are full of hints, ideas and tricks to help you use your machine to its fullest capacity.

Don't be afraid of the new machine. It really is as simple as 1-2-3-4-5:

1. Measure the ingredients and put them into the pan in the order specified (DAK and Welbilt read recipes from yeast up).
2. Choose the cycle and the setting.
3. Push the start button.
4. Check the dough after about 5 minutes of kneading to ensure that the dough has formed a round, smooth ball.
5. Remove the fully baked loaf of bread from the machine 2 to 4 hours later depending on what machine you have.

Perhaps the single most important thing to check is the consistency of the dough after 5 to 10 minutes of kneading. Many machines have a viewing window but if yours does not, don't be afraid to open the lid briefly during the kneading process. Open it only long enough to check the consistency and then to make any adjustments necessary. Don't leave the lid open long and don't open it during the baking cycle.

There are variables which must be addressed whether bread is made by hand or by machine. The flour and other ingredients pick up the moisture from the air. The moisture content of the grain berries themselves may vary as will the absorbency of whole grain flour (wheat, rye, etc.) according to how it was milled. As a result, the dough may have too much liquid, which could result in an overflow or a sunken top.

If you read recipes for making bread by hand, you will note that there is usually a range of flour (for example, 3 to 3½ cups). The directions will say something about kneading in the flour a little at a time until the dough is smooth. As recipes were developed for bread machine use, attempts have been made to provide exact ingredient amounts which will work each and every time. As in baking bread by hand, baking by machine does require some attention to the dough. The dough must be watched during the kneading process for variables, such as extra moisture in the flour from humidity or even from the way flours absorb the moisture due to the milling process.

When kneading dough by hand, you develop an ability to *feel* the right consistency. When kneading dough by machine, you can *see* the right consistency. If you have problems with consistency, allow the machine to knead the dough for approximately 5 minutes and then look at the dough. With few exceptions, it should form a nice, smooth ball. Sometimes the ball will be round and other times, it may take on more of a cylindrical shape which "tornadoes" up the side.

By watching the dough on a regular basis, you will soon develop a sense for what looks right. If you stick your finger in and touch it, it should feel moist but not really be sticky. Dough which is too dry will not mix properly or it may cause the machine to struggle (you'll hear it). It may be uneven (not smooth) or have two or more "balls" of dough. If this is the case, simply add whatever liquid you are using, one tablespoon at a time, until the required consistency is obtained. Conversely, dough which is too wet will not be able to form a ball, and flour should be added one tablespoon at a time.

If you hear the paddle rotating, but the ingredients on top of the dough are not moving, check to see that the paddle is inserted properly. Sometimes either the paddle was not placed on the kneading shaft correctly or it has slipped. The easiest way to check is to turn off the machine, reach in and feel whether the paddle is on correctly — it can usually just be pushed harder onto the shaft and the machine restarted without any difficulties (except a messy hand!).

Some ingredients which provide liquid (fruits, cottage cheese) may have a harder time initially being kneaded into the dough. It is helpful to take a rubber spatula, scrape down the sides of the pan and push the ingredients toward the kneading paddle. Once the paddle has picked up all ingredients, let it knead by itself for about 5 minutes and then check the dough consistency again for a smooth dough ball. If the process has taken quite a long time, you may wish to turn off the machine and start it again. This gives the dough a longer kneading with the correct consistency.

Because the moisture must be pulled out of fruit, vegetables or cheese, it may require a longer period of kneading before a judgment can be made as to whether to add more liquid. If lumps of the fruit, vegetable or cheese are still visible, chances are that you should let it knead longer before you add water. If you add water too early, you may end up with dough that is too moist. Should this happen, you need to add flour, a tablespoon at a time, until a smooth ball of dough is obtained.

When testing loaves using cottage cheese, we found that placing the yeast and flour in the machine first resulted in greater ease in mixing the ingredients together. All machines may have flour placed in the pan first if baking right away and not using a timer. Generally, recipes which have ingredients such as cottage cheese should be checked during the kneading and should not be set on a timer anyway because the cheese is perishable.

HINTS AND IDEAS SHARED BY BREAD MACHINE OWNERS
Basic Machine Tips

- If breads don't seem to rise well on a consistent basis, try moving the machine. It could be sitting in a draft. **D.C.**
Don't place the machines directly next to windows, open doors or heating/air conditioning vents for this reason. Some people have indicated that their machines did not work well next to the refrigerator.

- Help warm ingredients by running hot water into the pan and then drying prior to measuring ingredients. **B. M.**

- I add the oil to the pan prior to inserting the kneading paddle so that it won't stick. **J.C.**

- For heavier grains such as whole wheat, rye, corn or oats, allow the machine to knead the first time. Stop the machine (reset button or unplug) and start over. This gives the dough a longer kneading to develop the gluten structure. **P.S.**

- If you have a Zojirushi S-15 machine, if you want to stop and restart the machine, press the "restart" button. This stops the whole cycle and the 10-minute power outage protection is voided. **R.Y.**

- I had a problem with the top of the bread collapsing. I noticed that the tops leaned toward the back of the canister and at the back is the metal cooling blower (DAK and Welbilt ABM 100). I placed some aluminum foil over it and directed the air to blow up toward the top of the glass dome and this really helped. Now I only see a flat top once in awhile. **C.F.**

- Bread dough rises quicker in warmer weather. If your breads are rising and then collapsing, increase the amount of salt used to slow down the rise. **D.M.** says that she had failure after failure in the heat of the summer last year until she started using her "bread rapid" mode which is the fast, quick or turbo cycle. Watch the dough ball for extra moisture picked up from the air by the flour. Add extra flour a tablespoon or two at a time until you have a nice, round dough ball.

- Check the accuracy of the liquid measuring cup which may come with a bread machine. Mine was off by one tablespoon so I applied a strip of masking tape to the side of my liquid measuring cup and marked off the proper measurements by adding water to the cup. **R.Y.**

- Using an electronic air cleaner will negatively affect any yeast baking, whether by hand or machine. If using a bread machine and an air cleaner, turn the air cleaner off. **R. D.**

- I had one lopsided loaf and noticed that the low spot was on the side of the machine close to a window when it was very cold. I honestly believe it was in a draft. **S.U.**

- -Heat liquids to lukewarm (baby bottle) and add yeast to liquid. Add all other ingredients as usual and allow the machine to sit for 5 minutes before starting machine. This allows the yeast to proof (activate) before starting to knead.
-Do not use measuring spoons or cups provided with machine for recipes which do not come with the machine. The measurements are inaccurate.
-If using dried whole cherries, check for and remove pits first to avoid damaging the machine.
-Use a little less yeast if using the faster variety.
-Buy a small notebook and keep a log of recipe results and any adjustments you made.
-Never use an unfamiliar recipe on the timer until you have observed the kneading and baked it once.
-If you wrap cooled bread in plastic which subsequently "fogs up" from moisture, wrap a paper towel around the loaf and rewrap in plastic film. **A.R.W.**

A.W. has a Sanyo but many of his hints also apply to other machine owners. Even if you don't place the yeast directly in the water, you will get a better rise if your liquid temperature is lukewarm or room temperature. Do not use milk, juice or water directly from the refrigerator.

- When using a recipe for the first time, always wait and observe both mixing cycles. We made some oatmeal bread for the first time, and the first cycle was OK, so we left for a walk. When we got back, we heard the machine laboring through the second cycle and smelled smoke! We had to unplug the auto bakery before it burned up the motor. Apparently, the water got soaked up by the oatmeal over a period of time, and the mixture was much too dry for the second mixing. Also, cut bananas may not mix well; push them down to the paddle with a mixing spoon. **P.D.**

- If traveling and you want to take your bread machine, simply place all dry ingredients in a zip lock bag. Put a label on the bag saying how much water or liquid ingredients to use. A nice, easy way of making your own mix. Of course you could simply buy one of the premade mixes too. **R.K.R.**

- If you are concerned about scratching the inner pot of your bread machine with nuts (or Grape Nuts), chop the nuts, remove the dough before baking, knead the nuts into the dough by hand and bake in a conventional oven. **A.R.W.**

- Because I store my flour in the refrigerator, it picks up moisture and settles. I measure 90% of the flour, warm it in the microwave for a minute of so, sift and then measure. The warmer and sifted flour seems to result in a lighter loaf. **R.W.**

- Five gallon plastic drums used by many restaurants are perfect for storing up to 25 lb. flour. Many restaurants just throw these away and may be happy to give them to you if you ask! I have paid up to $10 for the same drums through mail order catalogs or hardware stores. **L.W.**

- When I open a jar of applesauce to use as a fat substitute, I freeze the leftovers in an ice cube tray. Then I can just defrost a small amount for the bread recipe. **M.O.**

- I find that warming margarine and using eggs brought up to room temperature is good; also water should be lukewarm. **S.A.S.**

- When using the National/Panasonic quick bread cycle, place parchment paper on the bottom of the pan to avoid sticking. Use boxes of prepackaged quick bread mixes such as blueberry muffin mix. **D.R.**
  These machines have a quick bread cycle which is used for batter which has been already mixed together. It is essentially used to bake the quick breads only so that your large oven need not be heated.

- My family loves *Grape Nut Bread* but the Grape Nuts scratched the bottom of the machine pan. I now mix the Grape Nuts (or sunflower seeds or nuts) with the flour before I put them in the machine and they do not scratch the pan anymore. **E.M.**

- I keep a small notebook with a record of every loaf of bread I make, what I put in, how it came out and who I gave it to. I cleaned out a couple of cupboard shelves above the machine and keep everything I use there with the exception of yeast and other refrigerated items. I also bought extra measuring cups, spoons and measuring bowls just for my bread baking. **E.F.**
  You can also keep a measuring spoon in each container for ease.

- The tall Rubbermaid container #7 (21 cups) is just the right size for a 5 lb. bag of flour. **N.B.**

- If using a Panasonic or National machine with a yeast dispenser, wait for the yeast to drop before opening the lid to add the raisins. Otherwise the yeast won't drop. **J.C.**

Crust Treatment

- Brush melted butter over the warm crust of the bread to prevent it from getting tough or hard. My grandson who hates eating crust will eat mine treated like this. **B.L.**

- For a soft crust, brush the bread with melted butter as soon as it is finished baking. Wrap it in plastic wrap as soon as it is cool. **D.M.**

Cutting and Storing the Bread

- It is easier to cut the bread into thin slices and avoid a lot of crumbs by refrigerating the bread before slicing. **M.J.**

- Use a good serrated knife, electric or hand, and gently saw through the bread without pressing down on it. **E.H.**

- I remove the paddle from my bread using a chopstick and I store the bread in an ice bucket! **B.E.**, DAK owner

- I use my electric carving knife to slice bread — the results are neat, even slices and can even be thin! **J.M.**

Cleaning the Machine and the Pan

- Use a computer keyboard attachment for a vacuum cleaner to clean the inside of the machine. **C.S.**

- Use a baby bottle nipple brush to clean the center portion of the kneading paddle. Spray it with nonstick vegetable spray to prevent sticking. **M.V.**

- Heat the handle of an old toothbrush enough to be able to bend the head to an angle that gets into the corners for cleaning the inside of the machine. The toothbrush loosens the encrusted bread which can then be vacuumed easily. **D.C.**
- Take the lid off the machine for cleaning and use a blow dryer periodically to blow crumbs out. Then just wipe it with a damp cloth. **K.G.**
  Not all machines have removable lids.
- I have never enjoyed an appliance so much!! I sprayed the top (inside) of the lid with Pam but now the lid is a mess and the screen has some blockage. **M.W**.
- Use dental floss to clean around the kneading paddle or other difficult-to-clean areas. **L.H.**

Ingredients and Substitutions

- Warm milk, water or other liquid in a microwave for about one minute or until it feels warm to the inside of your wrist — about 110° to 115°.
- Cut butter or margarine into quarters for better and easier distribution. Some manufacturers recommend placing butter in the corners of the pan to help in the even distribution. I just cut the butter up cold from the refrigerator and throw it into the pan — it softens during the kneading.
- If measuring honey, maple syrup, molasses or similar sweeteners, measure the oil first. By using an oiled measuring spoon the honey, etc., will simply slide right out of the measuring spoon.
- Bananas should be very ripe and may either be mashed or simply cut into small, 1-inch slices.

- Cheese should be lightly packed in the measuring cup.
- Do not use flours which come directly from the refrigerator or freezer. Flour which is cold and is in direct contact with the yeast before being warmed will slow the yeast, resulting in a small, low rising loaf of bread.
- Eggs and butter may be used directly from the refrigerator but all other ingredients should be warmed.
- Measure flour in solids measuring cups so it can be easily leveled. Measure liquids in measuring cups designed for liquids. If you slightly mismeasure something, it can be adjusted when you check the consistency of the dough.
- Use an egg yolk, white or 2 tbs. egg substitute for half eggs. There is a natural protein (lecithin) in the egg yolk which acts as a dough conditioner and helps breads to rise a little better.
- In general, sugar feeds yeast and helps it rise better. However, there is a fine line between the right amount of sugar and too much. Breads with large amounts of sugar, dried fruits or other sweet substances may actually be lower rising than those with less sugar. You may notice this if you make a plain loaf of white bread one day and use the same recipe the next day with a cup of raisins — the raisin bread will not rise as high.
- Different flours may react differently depending on the brand, the original wheat from which they were milled and the milling process itself. Try different brands of flour to see which you prefer.
- As a diabetes sufferer with high blood pressure and high cholesterol, **D.T.** has learned to make some substitutions in her bread baking. She uses a nutradiet pancake syrup instead of

honey and has also tried fruit spreads without sugar. She also substitutes a cooking oil low in saturated fat mixed with *Butter Buds* for butter or margarine. *Butter Buds* may be purchased at grocery stores.

- Use vegetable water (water in which vegetables such as potatoes, broccoli, etc. have been cooked) to add extra nutrients and flavor to the bread. **K.B.**
  The starch in some vegetables such as potatoes helps to give breads a better rise.

- I find I have great luck with almost any recipe if I use liquid buttermilk. It must have some magical property that makes the bread maker work so well. **L.H.**
  Baking soda is usually added to recipes with buttermilk or sour cream to offset some of the acidity. You can use 1/4 to 1/2 tsp. per loaf.

- Substitute applesauce for butter or oil in recipes, tablespoon for tablespoon. **D.L.**

- After suffering from several loaves with sunken tops, and going through the many salt/sugar changes, it became clear that the culprit was milk with acidophilus cultures. When I switched from sweet acidophilus milk to dry milk, the bread has a raised, brown top. **P.M.**

- We have recently been plagued by a series of failures during which the bread would rise beautifully but would collapse during the second rise, resulting in a baked brick. We varied the recipes according to all the hints to no avail. Water in our area often contains a high concentration of purification chemicals which were apparently killing the yeast. We switched to bottled spring water and since then every one of our loaves of bread has baked perfectly! **G.T.**

- If milling flour at home using an electric mill, wear ear plugs which are available at any drug store. An important house rule: the person milling the flour must wear ear protection and no one else is allowed in the room at the time, especially the children.

- If you store flour in the refrigerator, simply microwave a few seconds to bring it up to room temperature. Also, if you have tots who are fussy eaters, make breads with foods they will not normally eat "hidden" inside. **C. H.**

- I have been unable to purchase quinoa flour but the whole grain is available. I place the whole grain in my small food processor resulting in a good substitute for purchased flour. I also add ¼ cup of the whole grain for added texture and excitement as they pop when the bread is toasted. **R. L.**
  I would be very hesitant to mill grain in a blender or food processor as the motor may not be strong enough.

- Saffron is very expensive and is so often used to color the bread. I use an egg yellow food coloring to give the bread that nice rich color instead. **Mrs. E.E.**
  I often use food coloring to make bread fun for the kids. At Christmastime, we made a loaf of red and a loaf of green and used a slice from each to make sandwiches. Coordinate colors with other holidays or just for fun!

- As a Mormon who does not drink coffee, I substitute postum granules in recipes calling for instant coffee granules. The postum, which is a derivative of barley, gives the breads a nice, dark color and the bread turns out nice and moist. **K.M.**

- Spices may be adjusted to taste without affecting the remaining ingredients. Also, if your machine has a crumb tray, be sure that you don't put it in backwards as the pan won't go in properly. **A.W.**

- My husband has an allergy to milk and milk protein. For powdered dry milk, I substitute soya powder in an equal amount. It can be found in health food stores. It increases the nutritional value of the bread and does not alter the flavor. Also, when I use the rapid rise cycle on my Hitachi 201, I add 1 tsp. to 1 tbs. of vital gluten per cup of flour. I find this helps the bread to fully rise even when I use all bread flour. **A.K.**

- If you are watching your fat intake closely, try this: In addition to substituting applesauce for fat on a one-to-one basis, add 1 tsp. powdered pectin (Sure Gel or equivalent) to every large loaf of bread (½ tsp. for small and ¾ tsp. for medium.) The added pectin keeps the bread moist and thin slices do not even crumble when making sandwiches. **M.O.**

- I have been told that gluten flour is 80% gluten, not 50%. It really helps low-rising loaves, but it is expensive. I have discovered that lecithin is even better. I used to make the 3 cup *Peanut Butter and Jelly Bread* (Book I) to get a good sized loaf. With 2 teaspoons of lecithin, the 2-cup loaf is just as large and uses less ingredients and would, therefore, be lower in calories per slice. **A.W.**
Lecithin is a naturally occurring nutrient found in soy beans and in egg yolks which is often used as a dough enhancer in yeast breads (1 to 2 tsp per loaf). You can find lecithin granules at most health food stores.

- Use liquid *Butter Buds* instead of margarine to cut down on cholesterol and fat. **E.P.**

- Eggs help to give a better rise in breads. An egg may be added to the liquid by placing it in the bottom of the liquid measuring cup and then adding the liquid to it as needed to equal the recipe amount. The egg should not be microwaved but the liquid should be warmed before the exact measuring — otherwise the egg will cook when microwaved.

- Try using baby food when a puree is called for in a recipe. **M.M.**

- If a recipe calls for buttermilk powder, try a powdered buttermilk salad dressing blend — it adds flavor to the bread. **P.H.**

- When a recipe calls for raisins or nuts, I put them in a Pyrex cup, covered, into the microwave, and heat for about 20 to 30 seconds. This helps to warm them up and softens them. **S.M.**
- I tried to make apricot bread using all-fruit jam only to learn (through trial, error and studying books) that the bread needed actual sugar to rise. The sweetener/complex carbohydrate is not enough in the jam. **T.S.**
  About a year and a half ago I did quite a bit of testing and research into using fruit juice concentrates as the sweetening agent for breads. I, too, had miserable luck with the rising but did discover that the concentrates substituted nicely for the fat in the bread. The natural occurring pectin gives the bread a soft crumb and is a natural preservative (as is honey).
- Lightly sprinkle raisins (or similar dried fruits) with a little flour so they don't stick to each other as much. **C.J.**
- Add the raisins at the beginning of the second kneading cycle instead of at the beep.

TROUBLE SHOOTING GUIDE

Many of the standard techniques used for trouble shooting in baking bread by hand do not apply to machine baking for the simple reason that the bread machine cycles are all preprogrammed. Unless you have a Welbilt 150R or Zojirushi BBC-S15 programmable machine, you cannot tell the machine to let the dough knead or rise a little longer (or shorter). It becomes necessary to adjust the ingredients themselves to compensate for the lack of programmability in the machines.

Bread rises and then collapses: If the bread rises well but then collapses during baking, it is either rising too fast (cut sugar and/or increase salt or use a shorter cycle) or the size of the recipe is too large (use a smaller size recipe or cut the amount of flour and liquid).

Breads have a sunken top: Too much moisture in the dough may cause a sunken top. This may be because there is too much liquid in the recipe or because the flour has absorbed excess moisture from the air during very humid conditions. Cut back the amount of liquid by 1/4 and add it in slowly as the machine is kneading. Stop adding it when the dough forms a smooth round ball.

The crust is too hard or too dark: If you are baking on "light" or cannot control it, cut the amount of sugar, which darkens the crust, or remove the bread about 5 minutes before the baking is done.

The crust is too heavy or chewy: Brush butter or oil on the loaf while it is still hot. Salt crisps the crusts so you may wish to decrease the salt. Milk will give a softer crust than water.

The bread is not rising sufficiently: Increase the proportionate amount of white bread flour to other types of flour; cut salt, add 1 1/2 tsp. to 2 tbs. of vital gluten, increase liquid by a tablespoon or two.

The bread is not rising and/or is doughy (not baking properly) and heavy: This sounds like a "too much sugar" problem. Natural sugars are found in fruits and sometimes too many dried or fresh fruits actually inhibit the rising of bread and cause the bread not to bake properly. Cut down on fruits and other sugary substances. Too much butter or fat may cause a similar problem and may also be cut. While this may happen with any machine, it seems to happen more often with the glass domed machines. You may also place a piece of aluminum foil over glass dome to maintain even heat, but do not cover air vents.

The bread is rising too high: Too large a recipe size, not enough salt (controls yeast growth) or too much sugar (feeds yeast).

There are air bubbles at the top of the bread: Caused by too much yeast — cut yeast.

The texture is too crumbly and falls apart when cut: Increase salt or decrease liquid (keeping the dough in a smooth ball).

The bread is too heavy and dense: Too much salt and/or too little sugar, or too little liquid. Or not enough gluten to develop a strong rise — increase ratio of bread flour or add 1½ tsp. to 2 tbs. vital gluten.

The machine sounds like it is struggling and has difficulty kneading: Dough may be too dry or heavy; add 1-2 tbs. liquid as needed.

The dough is bumpy in appearance or has more than one ball of dough: Dough is too dry. Add tbs. of liquid at a time while machine is kneading until the dough forms a round, smooth ball.

The dough is very liquid and cannot form a ball: Dough is too wet. Add 1 tbs. flour at a time while the machine is kneading until the dough forms a round, smooth ball.

Raisins and similar ingredients do not mix in properly if added at the beep, but if added at the beginning, they become crushed: Lightly flour any dried fruits to prevent sticking. Add raisins at the beginning of the second kneading cycle if they are properly distributed.

QUESTIONS AND ANSWERS

I recently bought *The Bread Machine Cookbook*. Can the recipes be made by hand or in a food processor? M.A.

All recipes may be made by hand as well as by machine. I do not provide directions for making bread by hand but know of several people who bake the recipes conventionally. In fact, several heavy-duty mixer and food processor owners have commented that the recipes are given in just the right sizes for using their machines to knead the dough. They no longer have to make the conversions from other recipes!

Many recipes call for one package of yeast. How much is that? R.S.

One package of yeast equals 2¼ teaspoons or a scant tablespoon of yeast. I find that using half a package is generally sufficient for any size loaf in the bread machine. Experimenting with the type and amount of yeast in your machine will help you decide what is best for you.

Can breads using baking powder be changed to yeast? D.T.

Most breads using baking powder as a leavener have a higher amount of sugar than the yeast can tolerate. Yes, the breads can be adapted but it takes many trials and adjustments and will be only vaguely reminiscent of the baking powder loaf.

How can I use carrot or apple pulp in my bread? J.C.

When you use a juicer and want to use the pulp for breads, be sure to remove any sour tasting part of the fruit or vegetable you put in the juicer. For example, remove the outer layer of orange prior to juicing. Any pulp may be added to the bread dough. As the pulp will add liquid to the dough, adjust your liquid accordingly. One thing you may wish to do is to place the pulp in your liquid measuring cup prior to measuring the liquid. If using fruits high in pectin you could decrease or omit the fat (oil or butter). As always, watch the dough and adjust the flour or liquid if necessary.

My daughter is milk-intolerant and I hate to be limited to recipes not requiring the dry milk. May I substitute soy powder and if so, should I decrease the oil? K.C..

I would try using tofu milk powder. While I have not tested this as a substitution, I did test with it as a dough enhancer and found I liked the results. Tofu milk powders are available from health food stores. Keep in mind that you can substitute any kind of juice or water for milk in any recipe. In addition, if the recipe calls for only a tablespoon or two of powdered milk, it may simply be eliminated.

How long does the bread last before it goes bad? K.L.

Homemade breads do not contain any artificial preservatives. Both honey and fruit juices high in pectin are natural preservatives. The bread should be completely cooled and then wrapped in plastic and stored and should last a few days. Some people say they refrigerate it and others say it spoils quicker if refrigerated — I keep it wrapped on the kitchen counter.

I was recently told that I could get cancer by eating whole wheat flour as purchased in stores because it can become rancid and that I should only use fresh, home milled flour. Is this true? D.M.

It distresses me to think that someone is spreading this kind of false information in an attempt to sell a flour mill. I am not aware of any medical data supporting such a claim. Freshly milled whole wheat flour has some of natural oils left in the flour itself and should be refrigerated or frozen if not used right away. During the commercial milling process many natural oils are washed out, giving the flour longer shelf life. Many flour companies still recommend refrigerating flours for longer storage.

If ½ egg is optional, can I substitute molasses for it? C.M.

I have never heard of substituting molasses for eggs. The only reason I would consider this is because both provide moisture to the bread. If you don't want to use the egg, I would probably replace it with about 2 tablespoons of whatever liquid you are using. Too much molasses or sweetener may actually interfere with the rising power of the yeast.

How do you make a very dark rye bread? All I can find is "medium" rye flour. C.M.

Medium rye is usually found in grocery stores. Some health food stores may sell a darker rye flour. Many bakeries and bread companies "dye" the bread using molasses and/or burnt sugar. Coffee granules and/or unsweetened cocoa are often used in home bread baking to help achieve a darker colored rye bread.

Can I put coarse salt on top of a loaf? If so, when? R and D.

Yes, place it on top of dough towards the end of the second rising, just before baking. Be careful not to spill it outside the container. You may want to "wash" the bread first by very lightly brushing the top with some water or egg white which will help the salt stick to the bread.

I don't see much gluten flour used in your recipes. Why? N.P.

Gluten flour is a 50/50 combination of all-purpose flour and vital gluten. I much prefer using a tablespoon of 100% gluten which is sold as vital (wheat) gluten.

What is the difference between the following whole wheat flours? S.G.

whole wheat flour - flour milled from wheat which contains the bran and the germ.

stone ground whole wheat flour - whole wheat flour that has been milled between stones rather than steel.

whole wheat bread flour - whole wheat flour from a higher protein wheat, also called hard wheat.

whole wheat graham flour - different name for whole wheat flour.

whole wheat pastry flour - whole wheat flour from a soft or lower protein wheat, generally used for cakes and pastries.

Many of the recipes in your books call for water and powdered dry milk. I have on hand a quantity of sour milk (whole) that I would like to use. May I substitute the sour milk for both the water and dry milk powder? If so, should I add bicarbonate (baking soda) to bring up the pH level? P.G.

Buttermilk or sour milk may be substituted for any liquid in recipes on a cup to cup basis and baking soda should be added - about ½ tsp. per cup of milk. Buttermilk may act as a dough enhancer and cause the bread to rise too high. Check the dough towards the end of the second kneading. If it is too high, simply take a bamboo skewer and pierce the dough in the middle to let some air escape. Baking soda is not necessary with dried buttermilk powder.

I made your *New York Rye* (Book I) bread and it barely rose at all. The taste was great, but why did it fail? P.L.

Some breads are very low rising and heavy textured. Is it necessarily a failure if it does not rise to the top of the pan if you like the taste? To obtain a higher rising, lighter textured loaf with a different flavor, decrease the salt by one half, increase the sugar by ⅓ and add 1-2 tbs. vital gluten with the flours.

How do I measure fractions of eggs? E.C.

I find it easy to use either an egg white (lower in cholesterol) or yolk (contains lecithin for dough enhancement) for ½ egg. Egg substitutes may easily be used for fractions of eggs:

1 tbs.	= ¼ egg	2 tbs.	= ½ egg	3 tbs.	= ¾ egg
1⅓ tbs.	= ⅓ egg	2⅔ tbs.	= ⅔ egg	¼ cup	= 1 egg

I have a Panasonic 1½ lb. machine and the instructions say to add the dry ingredients first and then the wet ingredients. The yeast is placed in the yeast dispenser. Do I place the liquid or flour first for your recipes? C.G.

With the exception of the DAK and Welbilt machines, all machines, including Panasonic, are used to test recipes by placing the liquid in the pan first. The reason the DAK/Welbilt machines have the dry ingredients first is because the pan is inserted into the machine and sealed in place by the kneading paddle and the dry ingredients have less potential for leaking into the machine. The main concern with the order of ingredients is to prevent the yeast from coming in contact with the liquid ingredients until ready to activate. This is not a concern with a yeast dispenser.

I have a tremendous difficulty with the crust on loaves such as *Bread of the Dead* (what a name!) and other "cake-like" rich recipes (in a Panasonic 65 model). The crusts are usually a solid dark brown mass and the inside of the bread is usually fluffy to heavy. C.G.

Breads with high amounts of sugar such as you describe may tend to brown and have a thick, chewy crust. You may remove the bread from the machine about 5 to 7 minutes prior to the completion of the cycle to help avoid an overly brown crust or you may decrease the sugar by ¼ to ⅓ of the amount.

My dough never really forms a nice ball — it is usually an oblong mess. Is this normal? (Panasonic 65 model) C.G.

This happens if the ball of dough ends up on one side of the machine so that it rises very high on that one side and does not rise as high on the other side. Open the machine after the second kneading cycle and try to spread the dough out evenly in the pan.

I received a bread machine for Christmas and the bread is sometimes tough. What can I do? R.B.

Milk and butter both give bread a soft crumb and recipes which use both may work better for you. An egg may help also and if a recipe does not call for one, add it to the bottom of your measuring cup prior to measuring your liquid. This way, you'll be able to add the egg without adding too much liquid.

I notice very few recipes calling for yogurt. As many of us are very fat-conscious, can it be substituted for sour cream or buttermilk? L.S.

Yogurt may be substituted for either one — just keep an eye on the dough and adjust with yogurt or flour as necessary. Remember that ingredients such as yogurt used for liquid take longer to knead the liquid in properly and if you add water or more yogurt too soon, you may end up with too much liquid. Give it plenty of time to knead and start the machine over after 10 to 15 minutes of kneading if necessary. It is not necessary to use baking soda with yogurt.

I am unable to locate buttermilk powder that is called for in several recipes. Do you know where to purchase it? J.F.

I find *SACO* cultured buttermilk blend in the grocery store with the other dry milk products. Ask your grocer to carry it if they don't already, or call 800-373-SACO (business hours - Central Time) to find out where you can buy it in your area.

Do powdered egg substitutes (made from cornstarch, potato starch, guar gum, baking soda and powder) help bread to rise? A.W.

It is the lecithin in the egg yolks which causes the eggs to act as a dough enhancer. Baking soda and baking powder have mild leavening enhancing conditioners. If you want to add a dry enhancer, I would recommend using dried lecithin or vital gluten.

Several recipes call for walnut oil, but I can't find it at my grocery store. Where can I get it? E.W.

I use the brand *Loriva* which is found in most grocery stores in my area. If you have trouble locating it, call the company in New York at (516) 231-7940 to locate stores in your area. As usual, ask your grocer to carry items which you want. A good grocer would rather obtain items you request than have you go to other stores to find it.

My breads are not rising as high as I would expect. Why? S.W.

After a lengthy discussion, I discovered that S.W. has been freezing her flour for a longer shelf life. She was removing the flour from the freezer and placing it directly in the machine for baking. This low temperature would cause the yeast to slow down. If freezing or refrigerating ingredients, bring to room temperature prior to using. One way of doing this would be to place all ingredients in the pan as usual and set the timer for $\frac{1}{2}$ hour. Butter or margarine may be used straight from the refrigerator. In fact, I prefer using cold butter as it is easier to slice into tablespoons. I cut each tablespoon into thirds or quarters and drop the pieces into the pan. Liquids such as milk or juices which have been in the refrigerator are best warmed to "baby bottle" temperature (warm to inside of wrist) by using the microwave for 30 to 60 seconds. Eggs may be used at room temperature or straight from the refrigerator as long as your main liquid is warmed properly.

What is the recipe for Cornell flour? S.W.

The Cornell formula was devised by Dr. C. McKay of Cornell University to provide superior nutrition when using white (wheat) flour. He recommends placing 1 tbs. each of nonfat milk powder, soy flour and wheat germ in the bottom of each cup of flour and filling the cup with the white (wheat) flour. One cup equals 16 tablespoons, so that leaves 13 tablespoons or $\frac{3}{4}$ cup plus 1 tbs. flour.

	1 cup	**2 cups**	**3 cups**
nonfat milk powder	1 tbs.	$\frac{1}{8}$ cup	3 tbs.
soy flour	1 tbs.	$\frac{1}{8}$ cup	3 tbs.
wheat germ	1 tbs.	$\frac{1}{8}$ cup	3 tbs.
white flour	$\frac{3}{4}$ cup	$1\frac{1}{2}$ cups	$2\frac{1}{4}$ cups
additional white flour	1 tbs.	$\frac{1}{8}$ cup	3 tbs.

If recipes call for a liquid other than water, they turn out like bricks — why? R.L.

If recipes are not rising with milk or any liquid other than water, I would assume that the liquid is being used directly from the refrigerator. Warming liquids in the microwave for a minute or so until they reach lukewarm temperature will result in a better loaf of bread. I judge lukewarm to be comfortable to the inside of my wrist, much like the temperature for a baby bottle or approximately 110° to 115°. Some machines have a preheating cycle to bring all ingredients up to the proper temperature.

How can yeast dough be refrigerated for breakfast rolls or coffee cakes early the next morning? M.G.

There are two methods to do this:

1. Make your dough and allow the machine to knead it one time. Remove the dough immediately after the first kneading and turn off your machine. Place the dough in a (greased) plastic bag and seal shut but leave in enough air for the dough to rise. I like the inexpensive plastic bags without the zip lock for this. Place the bag in the refrigerator overnight or for the day. In the morning (or evening), remove the dough and shape into rolls or the coffee cake. Cover the dough with a warm towel and place in a warm, draft-free location for an hour or so until it has doubled in bulk and then bake as usual.

2. Make your dough on the dough cycle as normal allowing the machine to both knead and rise. Remove dough upon completion of cycle, place in a (greased) plastic bag with room for the dough to rise and place it in the refrigerator. Remove the dough from the refrigerator, shape and either warm as in step 1 or bake right away. This second method is perfect for pizza dough. You can always have pizza dough in the refrigerator for those evenings you don't feel like cooking. Remove the dough, roll it out cold, throw on some toppings and bake. Pizza is on the table in less time than a delivery would take! I generally do not grease the plastic bag for pizza dough but if a dough is particularly sticky, it helps to have a greased plastic bag for easy removal of the dough after the refrigerator rising. Instead of greasing, a light dusting of flour may be placed on the dough ball.

**You advise checking the dough after 5 minutes in the machine to adjust for moisture —
this completely eliminates the use of the timer or delay start. What do you suggest? M.S.**

If you have made a particular recipe several times and are comfortable with your weather conditions
and the recipe, the timer may be used without checking the dough and you should be okay. Keep in
mind that ingredients which sit in a machine on a timer for long periods of time in hot, humid weather
may pick up added moisture. You may wish to withhold a tablespoon of liquid or add a tablespoon of
flour under these conditions. The National and Panasonic machines which use the yeast dispenser
knead the dough the first time after programming the timer feature. This enables you to check the
consistency of the dough before the yeast is dropped into it just before the second kneading.

**DAK tells us to fold egg whites into the recipes instead of merely adding them. How can
you do this without touching the yeast, which is a no-no in machine bread baking? W.S.**

Beaten egg whites are sometimes used as a dough conditioner to help give breads a better rise. It
is very easy to fold egg whites into a dough by hand but the machine kneading will break down the
beaten eggs anyway. I generally just break the egg directly into the pan along with any other liquids.
While I generally warm liquids to "baby bottle" temperature, I will either bring eggs to room temperature
or use them directly from the refrigerator.

**The inside of some of the breads in my machine (DAK) do not cook through properly even
though I take the precaution of putting aluminum foil over the dome. W. S.**

This occurs mostly with breads containing high amounts of dried fruits (raisins), nuts or fat
(margarine, butter or oils). While it can happen with any machine, it seems to occur most frequently in
the machines with the glass domes (DAK or Welbilt ABM 100). First, use the sweet cycle (or oat/wheat
on the DAK Turbo IV) and place the aluminum foil over the dome while being careful not to block the

air vents. If that still does not correct the problem, cut the amount of fruit, nuts and fat in half. You may need to adjust the liquid slightly to adjust for less fat — watch the dough. High sugar content may also contribute to some breads not rising well and the same steps may be taken. If necessary, you may wish to run the bread machine through the *self help test* to make sure that everything is functioning properly. The directions are in your owner's manual or you should call DAK for directions.

I have often wondered what you do with all the bread that is made trying out new recipes. B.H.

That depends on where we are stationed at the time! When we were in California we lived in Navy Housing and my neighbors always devoured lots of bread. When we were stationed at the Naval Academy, my husband took bread to the midshipmen and I took bread to the Marine sentry guards who seemed to be able to eat an infinite amount of it. In Charleston, I give bread to a homeless shelter, the Ronald McDonald house, Meals on Wheels, the crew of my husband's ship (when in port) and to anyone who will eat it!.

I try using sprouted grains in my bread but I get a lot of caved in tops on the loaves. L.D.

Sprouts may vary greatly in the amount of moisture which they contain depending on which grains are sprouted, how fresh or old they are and when they were last watered. The best advice I have is to watch the dough for a smooth, satin dough ball. Adjust with water or flour 1 tablespoon at a time until your ball is formed.

INGREDIENTS
FLOURS AND GRAINS

Flours and grains are the most basic ingredients in bread. Wheat generally is the major ingredient in a loaf of bread. There are, however, a number of other grains and cereals which may be included in recipes. Each grain or cereal affects the taste, texture and rising abilities of a particular loaf of bread.

Amaranth grains are very small and may be used as is, sprouted or milled into flour. Amaranth is very high in calcium and low in calories. It has a slightly sweet and nutty taste. Use 2 tbs. in addition to every cup of flour or about ¼ cup of amaranth grains or flour to displace an equal amount out of each cup of flour.

Barley flour is usually what is used in bread baking. Use up to ¼ cup to displace an equal amount of each cup of flour. Barley is also sprouted, toasted and milled into diastatic malt which may be used as a dough enhancer — 1½ teaspoons to 1 tablespoon per cup of flour. Barley gives a malty taste to bread.

Most Americans equate **buckwheat** with pancakes but the flour will also add a strong, robust flavor to bread. Use 2 tbs. to ¼ cup to displace an equal amount of each cup of flour.

Cornmeal is readily available in grocery stores and is often used in bread baking. Meal is simply a coarser grind than flour and gives a slightly grainier texture. Corn flour may be milled at home or found in some health food stores or mail order catalogs. Cornmeal is generally milled from yellow, white and blue corn, each having slightly different nutritional values and flavorings. If you have your own flour mill, try milling dried Indian corn during the fall. The different colored corn makes for interesting changes in colored bread and in the flavoring. They are all interchangeable. Corn is very low in gluten and contributes to a low rise. Use up to ¼ cup to displace an equal amount of a cup of flour.

Kamut is an ancient variety of Egyptian wheat which has been revived and planted in Montana.

Kamut is very high in nutritional content but low in gluten. Use up to 1/3 cup to displace an equal amount out of every cup of flour.

Millet is also a very small grain which may be used as either the flour or the grain itself. Millet blends well with fruits (such as apple) and is slightly sweet itself. Use up to 1/4 cup to displace an equal amount out of every cup of flour.

Americans generally use **rolled oats** (such as Quaker) in bread baking. The only difference between instant and regular rolled oats is the thickness of the oats themselves and they are interchangeable in bread. Steel cut oats are the oat groats which are cut between steel rollers as opposed to rolling. Oat flour may be purchased or you may make it at home by processing one cup of rolled oats at a time in a good blender or food processor. Use up to 1/3 to 1/2 cup to displace an equal amount out of every cup of flour. Oats are low in gluten and contribute to a low rise.

Potato flour or **starch** may be used to give bread a moist crumb with a dry crust. Use 2 tbs. or 1/4 cup to displace an equal amount out of every cup of flour used.

Quinoa has a woodsy, nutty flavor. The grain itself is quite small and may be used whole or it may be milled into flour. Use about 2 tbs. in addition to each cup of bread flour.

Rice may be milled into flour using a home mill or 1/2 cup at a time using a blender with a very strong motor. Use up to 1/4 cup out of 1 cup of flour. Leftover cooked rice adds a nice moisture to bread and should be added with the wet ingredients. The water, milk or juice should be adjusted according to the moisture of the rice itself. Brown rice is more nutritious than processed white rice.

Rye is very low in gluten which means that bread with high amounts of rye will be low rising and dense but very flavorful. In bread machines, rye should not exceed 1/2 cup out of every cup of flour used. The addition of vital gluten (1/2 to 1 tbs. per cup of flour) may help in achieving a higher rising loaf of rye bread. Most Americans equate caraway seeds with rye breads although that need not be the case!

Spelt is another ancient grain which has recently been revived. It is possible to make a loaf of bread using no other flour other than spelt flour but it is very difficult to time in bread machines. For now, I would recommend using no more than 1/3 cup to displace an equal amount out of every cup of flour.

Triticale is a hybrid of wheat and rye. The flour may be difficult to obtain. Use it for up to 50% of total flour.

White flour, whether it is a bread flour, all purpose flour, pasta flour or pastry flour, is a wheat flour. That is, it is milled from wheat and is refined and processed so that all bran and germ are removed from the grain leaving only the white, starchy endosperm. **Whole wheat flour** is milled from wheat just like the white but the germ and bran are not removed in the process.

Flours which complement each other for taste, texture and nutrition include: amaranth and barley flours; brown rice and millet; cornmeal or flour and brown rice; triticale, rye or buckwheat; oat and soy; and buckwheat and quinoa. These combinations of flours or meals may be used for up to 1/4 cup to displace an equal amount out of every cup of flour.

The total cups of flour equivalents called for in most machines are approximately:

machine size	bread flour	various flours
1 lb.	2 to 2 1/4 cups	2 1/4 to 2 1/2 cups
1 1/2 lb.	3 cups	3 1/2 to 4 cups
2 lb.	3 1/2 to 4 cups	4 to 6 cups

YEAST

Yeast is one of the key ingredients in bread baking and may mean the success or failure of your loaf. Depending on how you buy it, it may be one of the most expensive ingredients in a loaf of basic bread so using the best yeast for the least price is of concern to all of us.

Over the last several years of working with bread machines and testing recipes, I have found it very difficult to compare apples to apples or should I say yeast to yeast and machine to machine. If the same recipe is loaded into two different machines in the morning and again in the afternoon, to what do I contribute an inch of loaf height? Is it the machine, the yeast, the change in ambient room temperature, or some other variable?

Recently, however, I have had the opportunity to work with seven identical machines and hold all other factors constant to test the various yeasts and amounts of yeast. Each machine was loaded with the identical recipe but different yeasts at the same time. Each experiment was repeated three times using the same (basic - not quick) cycle. All results were averaged. The rapid or quick rise yeast consistently resulted in higher rising loaves over those made with the regular dry active yeast. When testing the amount of yeast with 3 cups of bread flour (1½ lb. size), there was less than an inch height difference when using 2 tsp. of yeast versus 1 tsp. of yeast.

Yeast amounts may vary according to the type of flour being used and/or how sweet the bread is. I tested only white flour recipes. Whole grains and heavier grained breads (rye, oats, etc.) may need more yeast in general.

Yeast may respond more actively to a recipe which uses a large amount of sugar as compared to one with just a small amount.

The expiration date of the different types of yeast may also affect the outcome of a test like this. Since it was not possible to obtain yeast from different manufacturers with the same expiration date, I had to use what was available to me at that time.

Yeast responds to ambient temperatures. It may be necessary to increase yeast in colder weather or to decrease in very hot temperatures. These tests were done over the summer in South Carolina in an air conditioned environment. If you are uncomfortable changing yeast amounts, try using cooler liquids in hot weather.

Too much yeast may cause air pockets or air bubbles.

Compressed yeast is the same as cake yeast and is generally found in the refrigerated section of grocery stores. This yeast is not recommended for use in bread machines.

A rule of thumb from Red Star is to use ½ tsp. of yeast per cup of flour in the recipe.

Use lukewarm liquids unless your machine has a preheating cycle. I generally warm all liquids in the microwave for 1 minute so that it is comfortable on the inside of the wrist, or approximately 100°-115°.

Store open yeast in a tightly sealed plastic container in the refrigerator. If using yeast directly from the refrigerator, delay starting the machine for about 5 minutes to bring the yeast up to room temperature or allow the yeast to sit on the kitchen counter before measuring all other ingredients.

If you buy yeast in bulk, keep only a portion in the refrigerator and the remainder in the freezer. If the yeast has been frozen for longer than 6 months, proof the yeast to ensure that it is still active. Stir 1 tsp. sugar into ¼ cup lukewarm water. Add 1 tsp. yeast and stir gently. Let the mixture sit for about 5 minutes. You should get some bubbling action as well as a yeasty aroma.

LIQUIDS

Milk strengthens the gluten and gives bread a soft crumb. In addition, the fat in whole milk acts as a natural preservative. Water, skim, soy, goat or nut milks (coconut) may generally be substituted on a one-to-one basis. Nonfat dry milk is often used with water to add nutrition and a soft crumb to the bread. It is completely optional.

Bread which uses only **water** as the liquid (no fat, juice or powdered milk) tend to have a dry, crispy crust. Hard or alkaline water may affect the rising ability of the yeast, causing the bread not to rise sufficiently. Soft water may result in a sticky dough which likewise may not rise very well. If you notice that your bread suddenly is not rising, it could be that there has been a change in your drinking water. Try using bottled water to obtain better results.

Other liquids which may be used include any **fruit or vegetable juice, water in which vegetables or meats have been cooked, coffee** or **tea**. Liquids which are mildly acidic such as **potato water** or **buttermilk** may increase the leavening effect of the yeast, causing breads to rise higher. If using buttermilk, add 1/4 to 1/2 tsp of baking soda to your recipe.

Fruits and **vegetables** such as bananas, oranges, onions, etc., may be used for all or part of the liquid but the dough should be watched carefully for adjustments of water or flour during kneading. The natural sugars in many fruits used for liquids may affect the rising of the bread.

Eggs contribute liquid to the dough and add richness to the bread. Egg yolks contain lecithin which is often used as a dough enhancer. Beaten egg whites may also be used to assist in leavening the bread. Too many eggs may cause the bread to dry out too quickly.

DOUGH ENHANCERS

A dough enhancer is an optional ingredient which increases dough strength and makes a lighter-textured and often higher rising loaf of bread. Commercial bread bakers may use additives which are either unavailable to us or which we may not wish to use. There are, however, a number of natural ingredients which are available for bread machine baking.

Vital gluten is the protein which has been separated from wheat flour by rinsing off the starch. Recipes using 100% whole wheat flour or those which use a combination of bread flour along with flours or meals such as rye, cornmeal, oats, etc., may rise higher and/or have a better texture if vital gluten is added to the dough. Vital gluten may be found at health food stores or in some large grocery stores. Use 1 tsp. to 1 tbs. per cup of flour used. Use the higher amount of gluten with all purpose whole wheat flours (under 12% protein) or in loaves with a high percentage of nonwheat flours. Some stores sell gluten flour which is half (wheat) flour and half vital gluten. I find this product to be very expensive and it is not a direct substitute for vital gluten. If it is all you can find, put 1/4 cup in the bottom of your measuring cup when you measure in your regular flour.

Buttermilk is a low fat milk with active cultures similar to yogurt. Using buttermilk often results in higher rising, more tender loaves of bread. If substituting buttermilk for milk, water or juice, add 1/4-1/2 tsp. baking soda to counterbalance the acidity in the buttermilk. Along the same lines, a teaspoon of lemon juice or vinegar is sometimes added to bread dough to provide an acid which helps to increase the elasticity of the dough. This results in a light crumb and a higher rising loaf. Note that either lemon juice or vinegar are often added to regular milk as a substitute for buttermilk.

Ascorbic acid (vitamin C) is often added to commercially milled flours to help mature the flour and to improve its bread making qualities. Granular vitamin C may be found in some health food stores or through mail order. Tablets may be crushed using a mortar and pestle. Add approximately 125 mg. per cup of flour used.

Diastatic barley malt is made from sprouted barley. Malt is used to achieve a finer textured loaf of bread. While it may also be used as a sugar substitute when baking by hand and rising periods are variable, I find I prefer adding it to the dough as an enhancer when baking in a bread machine. I use 1/2-1 tbs. per cup of flour.

Lecithin is a natural substance found in both egg yolks and soy beans. Lecithin may be found in health food stores in a granular form which may be added to dough — 1 to 1 1/2 tsp. per cup of flour.

Eggs used in bread dough add to the structure and often result in higher rising, lighter textured loaves. This is due, I believe, to the lecithin in the yolks. If you want to add egg to a recipe, place it in the bottom of your liquid measuring cup prior to measuring your liquid.

Dough enhancer products are available in some areas. Some of the main ingredients are dried tofu powder which is a byproduct of soybeans and lecithin. Use 1 tsp. per cup of flour.

I have tried using **dried tofu milk drink powder** found in health food stores and have had fairly good results. I use 1 tbs. per cup of flour. Dried tofu by itself did not seem to make much difference.

Some bread bakers add a teaspoon of either **baking powder** or **baking soda** to the dry ingredients in order to help the yeast raise the dough. I had mixed results with both.

A word of caution in using dough enhancers — one of the main things to watch for is overflowing the pan of your bread machine. I strongly recommend watching the dough when experimenting with dough enhancers. If the dough starts to rise too high, take a sharp knife or skewer and pierce the loaf to deflate.

BREAD MACHINES

FEATURES

Basic white bread cycles may have one or two main kneadings depending on the manufacturer of the machine. Some machines have only a basic cycle which is used for all breads, whether sweet or whole grain.

Sweet cycles should be used with recipes containing 2 tbs. or more of sugar and/or fat (butter, margarine or oil). These cycles may have a longer rising time. The baking temperature is lower than the basic cycles for the higher sugar content of the breads.

French cycles may have a longer rising time but all have a higher baking temperature to crisp the crust.

Raisin cycles have a beep to indicate when to add raisins, nuts or other similar ingredients. Generally the beep is about 5 minutes before the end of the final kneading. The cycles may have a lower baking temperature (like the sweet cycle).

Whole grain cycles generally have longer kneadings and longer risings.

Dough cycles provide the initial kneading of the dough and one rise after which time the dough is removed from the machine, shaped, allowed to rise and baked in a conventional oven. This is the cycle used for bagels, rolls, pizza, etc. See the *Dough Cycle* chapter for specific information on how to use this cycle.

Timers enable the user to insert ingredients into the machine and to tell the machine when to have the bread ready, whether at 6:00 in the evening or 7:00 in the morning. Most timers have a 12 or 13 hour limit. With the exception of the Seiko 211 and the Welbilt ABM 600, all machines have a timer feature.

Preheating cycles are found on only a few machines. Basically the machine heats all ingredients to the proper temperature prior to starting the kneading cycle. As of now, the two machines with good preheating cycles are the National/Panasonic and West Bend machines.

Rapid/Quick/Turbo cycles are desired for quick yeast only and have shorter kneadings and risings. This cycle may be used in lieu of a basic white cycle.

Crust controls are usually buttons pushed when you start your machine, such as basic white, light setting. Some machines such as the DAK/Welbilt 100 machines have a knob which can be turned to control. The controls shorten or lengthen the baking time by about 5 minutes.

Power outage protection prevents a short (usually 10 minutes or less) loss of electricity from stopping the entire machine process. If this is not included with your machine and you have a loss of electricity, remove the dough and finish baking the bread conventionally.

Viewing windows are a nice feature if you like to frequently check the process of your bread machine baking. It is always a good idea to check the dough about 5 minutes into the initial kneading cycle to make sure that all is going well. If you don't have a viewing window, open the lid long enough to check the dough. Don't leave the machine open for long periods of time.

Cooling/warming cycles are found in many machines to either start cooling the bread or to keep it warm until it is removed from the machine. This is to prevent the bread from becoming soggy and wet if not removed as soon as the baking is completed.

MACHINE CAPACITY

In general, 1 lb. machines use 2 to 2¼ cups of bread flour or 2 to 2¾ cups of combination flours (bread, whole wheat, rye, oats, corn, etc.) Two and a half to 3 cups of whole grain flours may be used.

The 1½ lb. machines use 3 cups of bread flour or 3½ to 4 cups of a combination of flours such as bread flour, whole wheat, rye, oats, corn, etc. Up to 5 cups of whole grain flours may be used in most 1½ lb. machines without fear of overflows.

There are several 2 lb. machines which are being introduced as this book is written. The pans are generally vertical rectangles and should be 5 to 6 inches square with a height of approximately 9 inches. A full 2 lb. machine can use up to 4 cups of bread flour although I find that $3\frac{1}{2}$ cups usually results in a nice loaf of bread at or just over the lip of the pan. Four or 5 cups of combination flours (bread with whole wheat, oats, rye, corn, etc.) may easily be used and up to 6 cups of whole grain flours. Some machines are being introduced as 2 lb. machines but the size of the pan is the same as the $1\frac{1}{2}$ lb. pan and therefore, must use $1\frac{1}{2}$ lb. size recipes.

A few words about pushing the maximum flour capacity of your bread machine:

If at any time it sounds like the machine is struggling with a high amount of flour, add a tablespoon or two of water (or more if necessary) to soften the dough. If the machine is struggling, it could cause the motor to give out. Most machines have a built-in control to cause the motor to stop before serious damage is done.

The sides of the machine may require scraping to help get all ingredients to the kneading paddle. Once the dough has formed a ball it will do just fine and may be left. If it has taken the machine a long time to knead the ingredients into a ball, you may wish to stop the machine once the dough ball is formed and start it over from the beginning, giving it a longer knead.

One of the main concerns about using too much flour is overflowing the sides of the pan. Usually you will end up with a mushroom — the dough may cook onto the lid of the pan or perhaps the dough does not cook properly at the top. The real mess, however, is when the dough spills down the sides of the pan and gets all over the inside of the machine and on the heating elements. While this can be cleaned up (I've done it lots of times in testing), it is a messy, time-consuming chore. It is difficult to remove all dough from the heating elements but it burns off the next time the machine is used.

It is wise to check the dough during the second rise. If it looks too high, use a bamboo skewer (or similar) and pierce deep into the dough to deflate it. Do not use metal objects which could scratch the pan. If you have absolutely used the wrong size recipe and it is starting to overflow, remove a portion of the dough. This enables you to at least salvage something!

MACHINE MODELS AND SIZES

	recipe size	add raisins
Black and Decker	1½ lb. (1¾ lb.)	at beginning
Breadman (Seiko)	1¼ lb. (small pan)	at beep
Chefmate (see Seiko)		
Citizen (see DAK and Welbilt)		
DAK - all	1½ lb. or 1¾ lb.	at beep
Decosonic, see DAK and Welbilt	(machines expected in 1994)	
Hitachi 101, 102, 201	1½ lb. (1¾ lb.)	at beep
Hitachi 301	up to 2 lb.	at beep
Maxim	1 lb.	after 30 minutes
Mister Loaf (see Seiko)		
National/Panasonic 55 models	1 lb.	after 30 minutes
National/Panasonic 65 models	1½ lb. or 1¾ lb.	after first knead
Pillsbury (see Seiko)		
Regal K6771	1½ lb. (1¾ lb.)	at beep
Regal K6772	1 lb.	at beep

Regal K6773 (Seiko)	1¼ lb. (small pan)	after 10-12 minutes
Regal K6776 small pan	1½ lb. (1¾ lb.)	at beep
Sanyo 10, 11 and 12	1 lb.	at beep
Sanyo 15 (not yet tested)	1½ lb.	at beep
Sanyo 20 (not yet tested)	up to 2 lb.	at beep
Seiko 12	1 lb.	at beginning
Seiko 210	1 lb.	at beep
Seiko 211	1 lb.	after 10 minutes
Seiko 215 small pan	1¼ lb.	at beep
Seiko 520 (not yet tested)	up to 2 lb.	at beep
Singer (Seiko)	1¼ lb. (small pan)	after 10-12 minutes
Toastmaster 1150, 1151	1 lb.	at beep
Toastmaster 1152U, 1152T	1 lb.	at beep
Welbilt 100, 150R	1½ lb. to 1¾ lb.	at beep
Welbilt 300, 350, 500, 550, 600 or 800	1 lb.	at beep
West Bend	1½ lb.	at beep
Zojirushi S-15	1½ lb. (1¾ lb.)	at beep
Zojirushi N-15	1½ lb. (1¾ lb.)	at beginning

Recipe size in parentheses indicates that recipes were tested on this size but that it is necessary to keep an eye on the dough for proper mixing and to prevent excessive rising. Recipe size of 1¼ lb. (small pan) means that I tested these machines with 1½ lb. size recipes, but that because of the small pan it is necessary to keep an eye on the dough to prevent excessive rising.

Except for National/Panasonic 65 machines, all machines can make a smaller size recipe.

WHITE BREADS

FARMHOUSE WHITE BREAD

JOAN GARNEAU

Joan loves making this bread and says it has a surprise taste and crunch because of the sesame seeds. Use an egg yolk, white or 2 tbs. egg substitute for the half egg.

	1 lb.	1½ lb.	1¾ lb.
milk	⅔ cup	1 cup	1¼ cups
egg	½	1	1
butter	1 tbs.	2 tbs.	2 tbs.
salt	⅓ tsp.	½ tsp.	⅔ tsp.
sugar	1 tbs.	1½ tbs.	2 tbs.
bread flour	2 cups	3 cups	3½ cups
rapid or quick yeast	1 tsp.	1½ tsp.	2 tsp.
*sesame seeds	1½ tbs.	2 tbs.	2½ tbs.
flour equivalent	*2 cups*	*3 cups*	*3½ cups*
cycle	*raisin, white; no timer*		
setting	*medium*		

*Add seeds at the beep or appropriate time for your machine.

---

per 1 oz. *73 calories, 2.9 g protein, 11.7 g carbohydrate, 1.6 g fat, 9 mg cholesterol, 64 mg sodium*

STOLLEN

JOANNE BAUER AND CARYN GATES

Joanne and Caryn have adapted this recipe to fit their bread machines. This family recipe has been handed down through the generations since the 1880s. Joanne says that she sometimes substitutes rum or rum extract for the almond and adds a pinch of cardamom to it. If citron or candied red and green cherries are unavailable, use dried fruit mix. Breads with high amounts of fruits and nuts may have difficulty baking through properly in some machines. If that is the case, cut the amount of fruit in half and be sure to use a sweet cycle if available. This is a low rising bread and is almost cake-like in texture.

	1 lb.	1½ lb.	2 lb.
milk	½ cup	¾ cup	1 cup
eggs	1	1½	2
butter or margarine	2 tbs.	3 tbs.	4 tbs.
almond extract, or rum extract	¼ tsp.	⅓ tsp.	½ tsp.
sugar	¼ cup	⅓ cup	½ cup
salt	¼ tsp.	⅓ tsp.	½ tsp.
cinnamon	⅛ tsp.	¼ tsp.	⅓ tsp.
bread flour	2 cups	3 cups	4 cups

rapid or quick yeast	1 tsp.	1½ tsp.	2 tsp.
*raisins	¼ cup	⅓ cup	½ cup
*citron or dried fruit	¼ cup	⅓ cup	½ cup
*red or green cherries	¼ cup	⅓ cup	½ cup
*almonds, chopped	¼ cup	⅓ cup	½ cup
flour equivalent	*2 cups*	*3 cups*	*4 cups*
cycle	*raisin, sweet; no timer*		
setting	*light*		

*Add at the beep or appropriate time for your machine.

---

per 1 oz. *110 calories, 3 g protein, 17.6 g carbohydrate, 3.3 g fat, 14 mg cholesterol, 73 mg sodium*

EASY CHEESE BREAD

LORENA VENSEL

Lorena prefers using a Quatro Fromage blend of cheese in this but Swiss or freshly grated Parmesan are also tasty. When using a drier cheese such as Parmesan, liquid may need to be added. Watch the dough and adjust the consistency as required with water or flour. While the recipe calls for a multi-blend flour (found at health food stores), rye or oat flour may also be substituted. If the machine has difficulty kneading the ingredients initially (notorious with cheese breads), scrape the sides of the pan with a rubber spatula to help the ingredients get picked up by the kneading paddle.

	1 lb.	1½ lb.	1¾ lb.
milk	⅓ cup	½ cup	⅔ cup
water	⅓ cup	½ cup	⅔ cup
freshly grated cheese	⅔ cup	1 cup	1⅓ cups
sugar	2 tsp.	1 tbs.	1⅓ tbs.
salt	½ tsp.	1 tsp.	1 tsp.
dill weed	½ tsp.	1 tsp.	1 tsp.
multi-blend flour	½ cup	¾ cup	1 cup
bread flour	1⅓ cups	2 cups	2⅔ cups

vital gluten	2 tbs.	3 tbs.	1/4 cup
rapid rise yeast	1 1/2 tsp.	2 tsp.	2 tsp.
flour equivalent	*2 cups*	*3 cups*	*4 cups*
cycle	*white, sweet; no timer*		
setting	*light*		

---

per 1 oz.   *89 calories, 9.6 g protein, 13.3 g carbohydrate, 1.9 g fat, 5 mg cholesterol, 105 mg sodium*

SALLY LUNN

MAXINE FRAZIER

Maxine and her friend spent their vacation playing with their bread machines and sent me this recipe for Sally Lunn. I used only milk rather than water and milk. I warm the milk to lukewarm as usual. This is a high rising, sweet bread with a moist, soft dough which may climb the walls of the pan — like a tornado.

	1 lb.	**1½ lb.**	**2 lb.**
milk	⅔ cup	1 cup	1¼ cups
egg	1	1	2
butter or margarine	2 tbs.	3 tbs.	4 tbs.
salt	½ tsp.	1 tsp.	1 tsp.
sugar	¼ cup	⅓ cup	½ cup
bread flour	2 cups	3 cups	4 cups
rapid or quick yeast	1 tsp.	1½ tsp.	2 tsp.
flour equivalent	*2 cups*	*3 cups*	*4 cups*
cycle	*white, sweet; no timer*		
setting	*light*		

per 1 oz.   83 calories, 2.5 g protein, 12.9 g carbohydrate, 1.9 g fat, 1 mg cholesterol, 28 mg sodium

HAWAIIAN BREAD

CAROL SCLOVE

Carol finds bread baking to be a great hobby. Her recipe proves she has talent for it! One small can (6 oz.) equals ¾ cup of pineapple juice. One half egg equals 1 yolk or white or 2 tbs. egg substitute. This has been an often requested recipe!

	1 lb.	1½ lb.	1¾ lb.
pineapple juice	⅔ cup	¾ cup	1 cup
egg	½	1	1
vegetable oil	1½ tbs.	2 tbs.	2½ tbs.
honey	2 tbs.	2½ tbs.	3 tbs.
salt	½ tsp.	¾ tsp.	1 tsp.
bread flour	2¼ cups	3 cups	3½ cups
nonfat dry milk	1½ tbs.	2 tbs.	2½ tbs.
rapid or quick yeast	1½ tsp.	2 tsp.	2 tsp.
flour equivalent	*2¼ cups*	*3 cups*	*3½ cups*
cycle	*white, sweet; no timer*		
setting	*light*		

per 1 oz.   87 calories, 2.5 g protein, 15.4 g carbohydrate, 1.6 g fat, 0 mg cholesterol, 71 mg sodium

HAWAIIAN SWEET BREAD

PENNY GRANT

Penny fell in love with Hawaiian sweet bread while visiting a friend in Hawaii. When she couldn't find a recipe for it for her machine, she developed one herself! She uses Butter Crisco; I tested using margarine. One small can (6 oz.) of pineapple juice equals approximately ¾ cup. Water may be added to that if you don't want to open a second can. Orange juice may be substituted for a slightly different flavor. Use an egg yolk, white or 2 tbs. egg substitute for the half egg. This is a winner. If you have a 1¼ lb. machine (Seiko), make only the 1 lb. size to prevent overflows. This can be a high rising bread.

	1 lb.	**1½ lb.**	**2 lb. *only***
pineapple juice	⅔ cup	¾ cup	1 cup
egg	½	1	1
milk	3 tbs.	¼ cup	⅓ cup
butter or margarine	2½ tbs.	4 tbs.	4 tbs.
coconut or vanilla extract	1 tsp.	1 tsp.	1 tsp.
ground ginger	pinch	¼ tsp.	⅓ tsp.
salt	⅓ tsp.	½ tsp.	1 tsp.
sugar	¼ cup	⅓ cup	⅓ cup

potato flakes	1/3 cup	1/2 cup	1/2 cup
bread flour	2 1/2 cups	3 cups	3 1/2 cups
vital gluten, optional	2 tsp.	1 tbs.	1 tbs.
rapid or quick yeast	1 tsp.	1 1/2 tsp.	1 1/2 tsp.
flour equivalent	*2 2/3 cups*	*3 1/2 cups*	*4 cups*
cycle	*sweet, white; no timer*		
setting	*light*		

per 1 oz. *104 calories, 3 g protein, 18.3 g carbohydrate, 2.2 g fat, 0 mg cholesterol, 73 mg sodium*

QUICK POTATO BREAD

RUTH LEE

Ruth Lee makes this in her Hitachi on the rapid cycle using quick or rapid rise yeast. She says it lasts about 3 minutes with her two grandsons around! This is a simple bread to make when you use instant potato flakes. I cut back on her butter.

	1 lb.	1½ lb.	1¾ lb.
water	¾ cup	1¼ cups	1⅓ cups
butter	2½ tbs.	3 tbs.	3 tbs.
sugar	2 tbs.	2 ½ tbs.	2½ tbs.
salt	⅔ tsp.	1 tsp.	1 tsp.
potato flakes	1½ tbs.	2 tbs.	2½ tbs.
bread flour	2 cups	3 cups	3½ cups
rapid or quick yeast	1 tsp.	1½ tsp.	2 tsp.
flour equivalent	*2 cups*	*3 cups*	*3½ cups*
cycle	*white, sweet; timer*		
setting	*medium*		

per 1 oz.   73 calories, 1.8 g protein, 11.6 g carbohydrate, 2.2 g fat, 0 mg cholesterol, 116 mg sodium

POTATO BREAD

Pat says this is one of their standby breads and she makes it all the time. Cook the new or small potato in the microwave until soft and cut it into quarters or eighths (the machine will mash it during the kneading). Place the cut potato, peel and all, into the liquid measuring cup and add water up to the level given. She sometimes adds 1-2 tbs. buttermilk dressing mix (dry) for extra flavor.

	1 lb.	**1½ lb.**	**2 lb. only**
potato, cooked	4 oz.	6 oz.	7 oz.
water	as needed	as needed	as needed
wet ingredients should equal	1 cup	1½ cups	1¾ cups
butter	1 tbs.	1½ tbs.	2 tbs.
sugar	1½ tbs.	2 tbs.	2½ tbs.
salt	¾ tsp.	1 tsp.	1 tsp.
bread flour	2 cups	3 cups	3½ cups
yeast	1 tsp.	1½ tsp.	2 tsp.
flour equivalent	*2 cups*	*3 cups*	*3½ cups*
cycle	*wheat, sweet, white; no timer*		
setting	*medium*		

per 1 oz.   68 calories,   2 g protein,   12.8 g carbohydrate, 1 g fat, 0 mg cholesterol, 110 mg sodium

FINNISH PULLA (COFFEE BREAD)

JO ULVILA

Jo adapted this bread from her mother-in-law's recipe which she used to serve each afternoon with coffee. The men in the fields would listen for the whistle of the afternoon train at 3:00, the signal to go home for their coffee and pulla. It is usually made in a straight braid but may sometimes be shaped into a wreath for special occasions. Jo says that she sometimes adds a teaspoon of vanilla and some chopped citrus fruit for a slightly different flavor. This was tested as a loaf in the bread machines. If, however, you want to make this on the dough cycle, make the 1½ lb. size. Upon completion, remove the dough, divide it into three sections, braid it and let it rise for about 30 minutes. Bake in a preheated 375° oven for 25 to 30 minutes. Do not overbake as it will dry out.

	1 lb.	**1½ lb.**	**2 lb.**
milk	½ cup	¾ cup	¾ cup
egg	1	1½	2
butter	2 tbs.	3 tbs.	4 tbs.
sugar	¼ cup	⅓ cup	½ cup
salt	⅔ tsp.	1 tsp.	1 tsp.
ground cardamom	⅔ tsp.	1 tsp.	1¼ tsp.

bread flour	2 cups	3 cups	3½ cups
rapid or quick yeast	1½ tsp.	2 tsp.	2 tsp.

Glaze: Add ¼ cup sugar to 1 beaten egg and mix well. Brush on raised bread. Sprinkle sugar and poppy seeds or chopped or sliced almonds on the top and bake. If doing this in the machine, be very careful not to spill into the machine itself!

flour equivalent	*2 cups*	*3 cups*	*3½ cups*
cycle	*sweet, white; no timer*		
setting	*light*		

---

per 1 oz.   *80 calories, 2.3 g protein, 13.7 g carbohydrate, 1.8 g fat, 0.6 mg cholesterol, 115 mg sodium*

HOUSKA (BOHEMIAN SWEET BREAD)   JEAN ALLEN

Jean is not sure if her great grandma is appalled or applauding her efforts for adapting this old family recipe to the bread machine! She says that her mother sometimes adds golden raisins. This bread may appear to have too much liquid, but it is supposed to be very moist. It is traditionally braided.

	1 lb.	**1½ lb.**	**2 lb.**
milk	½ cup	1 cup	1 cup
eggs	1	1	2
butter	2 tbs.	3 tbs.	¼ cup
salt	½ tsp.	¾ tsp.	1 tsp.
sugar	3 tbs.	¼ cup	⅓ cup
mace	¼ tsp.	½ tsp.	½ tsp.
bread flour	2 cups	3 cups	3½ cups
rapid or quick yeast	1 tsp.	1½ tsp.	2 tsp.
flour equivalent	*2 cups*	*3 cups*	*3½ cups*
cycle	*sweet, white; no timer*		
setting	*light*		

per 1 oz.   *77 calories, 2.3 g protein, 12.9 g carbohydrate, 1.8 g fat, 0.6 mg cholesterol, 93 mg sodium*

BLUE CHEESE BREAD

RAMONA SCHALL

Ramona has made this bread (with the raisins) for years the old-fashioned way, and is now able to do it with the bread machine! Serve with tossed salad or soup. Watch the dough, scrape the pan sides and add flour or water if necessary.

	1 lb.	1½ lb.	1¾ lb.
milk	¾ cup	1 cup	1⅓ cups
butter or margarine	1 tbs.	1½ tbs.	2 tbs.
crumbled blue cheese	¼ cup	⅓ cup	½ cup
sugar	1⅓ tbs.	1½ tbs.	2 tbs.
salt	½ tsp.	½ tsp.	1 tsp.
bread flour	2¼ cups	3 cups	3½ cups
rapid or quick yeast	1½ tsp.	1½ tsp.	2 tsp.
*raisins, optional	⅓ cup	½ cup	⅔ cup
flour equivalent	*2¼ cups*	*3 cups*	*3½ cups*
cycle	*white, raisin; no timer*		
setting	*medium*		

*Add raisins at the beep or appropriate time for your machine.

---

per 1 oz.   146 calories, 3.2 g protein, 28.7 g carbohydrate, 2.2 g fat, 3.5 mg cholesterol, 132 mg sodium

CHEESE WINE BREAD

TERRY WARD

Terry says that this is her family's all time favorite bread — it's great with chili. She usually uses a pepper Jack cheese or adds a jalapeño or two to regular Monterey Jack. She likes to use Chardonnay, but has also used flat beer. If you prefer no alcohol, substitute water. Terry says she adds half of the cheese at the beginning and the other half at the beep in her Hitachi. I cut her butter amount in half.

	1 lb.	**1½ lb.**	**2 lb.**
wine, beer or water	⅓ cup	½ cup	⅔ cup
butter	2 tbs.	4 tbs.	5 tbs.
egg	2	3	3
cheese, shredded	½ cup	1 cup	1 cup
salt	½ tsp.	1 tsp.	1 tsp.
sugar	1½ tsp.	2 tsp.	2½ tsp.
bread flour	2 cups	3 cups	3½ cups
rapid or quick yeast	1½ tsp.	2 tsp.	2 tsp.
flour equivalent	*2 cups*	*3 cups*	*3½ cups*
cycle	*white, sweet; no timer*		
setting	*light*		

per 1 oz. 85 calories, 3.2 g protein, 10.8 g carbohydrate, 2.8 g fat, 4 mg cholesterol, 115 mg sodium

ENGLISH MUFFIN BREAD

JUDY SHROYER

Judy scalds the milk and stirs in the instant potato flakes to dissolve them. I am lazy and warm the milk as usual and then put both the milk and potato flakes in together so they mix in the machine.

	1 lb.	1½ lb.	2 lb.
milk	¾ cup	1⅛ cups	1⅓ cups
potato flakes	1½ tbs.	2 tbs.	2½ tbs.
unsalted butter	2½ tbs.	4 tbs.	5 tbs.
sugar	2 tsp.	1 tbs.	1⅓ tbs.
salt	¾ tsp.	1 tsp.	1 tsp.
bread flour	2 cups	3 cups	3½ cups
rapid or quick yeast	1 tsp.	1½ tsp.	1½ tsp.
flour equivalent	*2 cups*	*3 cups*	*3½ cups*
cycle	*sweet, white; no timer*		
setting	*light to medium*		

---

per 1 oz.   75 calories, 2.2 g protein, 11.5 g carbohydrate, 2.3 g fat, 5.7 mg cholesterol, 106 mg sodium

NEW HAMPSHIRE WHITE BREAD LOOSEY BLAKE

Loosey says that this is her favorite basic white recipe. Use scant measurements of the water. Loosey sometimes makes this into rolls and also enjoys the bread toasted.

	1 lb.	**1½ lb.**	**1¾ lb.**
water	¾ cup	1 cup	1¼ cups
butter or margarine	2 tbs.	2½ tbs.	3 tbs.
sugar	2 tbs.	2½ tbs.	3 tbs.
salt	1 tsp.	1 tsp.	1 tsp.
bread flour	2 cups	3 cups	3½ cups
rapid or quick yeast	1 tsp.	1½ tsp.	2 tsp.
flour equivalent	*2 cups*	*3 cups*	*3½ cups*
cycle	*white; timer*		
setting	*medium*		

---

per 1 oz.   *69 calories, 1.8 g protein, 11.7 g carbohydrate, 1.7 g fat, 0 mg cholesterol, 153 mg sodium*

FRUIT AND VEGETABLE BREADS

Bread recipes which use fruit or vegetables for some or part of the liquid must be watched carefully for the proper moisture content. The moisture content of the fruit or vegetable which you use may vary from one day to the next depending on the ripeness and freshness of the produce.

Fruit recipes also tend to be higher in sugar due to the fruit itself. If you have a sweet cycle or specific raisin cycle, use it for the lower baking temperature. If the bread has a doughy spot in the middle of the loaf, cut the amount of dried fruit or nuts in half the next time.

HONEY RAISIN CINNAMON BREAD   NORMA DAVIS STOYENOFF

Norma developed this recipe much to the delight of her family. The salt amounts given are half of what she submitted. Norma also uses more water than I found worked in most machines.

	1 lb.	**1½ lb.**	**1¾ lb.**
water	⅔ cup	1 cup	1⅛ cups
margarine or vegetable oil	2 tsp.	1 tbs.	1⅓ tbs.
honey	1½ tbs.	2 tbs.	3 tbs.
salt	½ tsp.	¾ tsp.	1 tsp.
cinnamon	1 tsp.	1½ tsp.	1¾ tsp.
whole wheat flour	⅓ cup	½ cup	⅔ cup
bread flour	2 cups	2½ cups	3 cups
rapid or quick yeast	1½ tsp.	2 tsp.	2 tsp.
*raisins	⅓ cup	½ cup	⅔ cup
flour equivalent	*2⅓ cups*	*3 cups*	*3⅔ cups*
cycle	*raisin, sweet; no timer*		
setting	*light*		

*Add raisins at the beep or appropriate time for your machine.

per 1 oz. *76 calories, 3 g protein, 14.7 g carbohydrate, 0.8 g fat, 0 mg cholesterol, 75 mg sodium*

HEAVENLY RAISIN NUT BREAD

LEE HICKNEY

Lee has been very creative in developing recipes for his bread machine. I slightly decreased the amount of butter he uses. This wet, moist dough rises very well.

	1 lb.	1½ lb.	1¾ lb.
water	⅔ cup	1 cup	1⅛ cups
egg, large	1	1½	2
butter or vegetable oil	2 tbs.	3 tbs.	¼ cup
molasses	1 tbs.	1½ tbs.	2 tbs.
sugar	2 tbs.	3 tbs.	3 tbs.
salt	1 tsp.	1½ tsp.	1½ tsp.
cinnamon	1 tsp.	1½ tsp.	1½ tsp.
bread flour	2 cups	3 cups	3½ cups
nonfat dry milk	2 tbs.	2½ tbs.	3 tbs.
rapid or quick yeast	1 tsp.	1½ tsp.	2 tsp.
*raisins	½ cup	⅔ cup	¾ cup
*chopped walnuts	½ cup	⅔ cup	¾ cup
flour equivalent	*2 cups*	*3 cups*	*3½ cups*
cycle	*white, sweet, raisin; no timer*		
setting	*light*		

*Add raisins at the beep or appropriate time for your machine.

per 1 oz.   115 calories, 3.3 g protein, 16.9 g carbohydrate, 4.2 g fat, 0 mg cholesterol, 141 mg sodium

CRANBERRY CORNMEAL BREAD

CARYN HART

Caryn is a veteran bread baker and has adapted many of her favorite recipes for the bread machine. She pours boiling water over the cornmeal before placing it in the machine. I take the lazy way and simply put it all in the machine at once. The cranberries should be coarsely chopped. They will add some liquid to the dough. As usual with any fruit like this, adjust the dough with flour or water if necessary.

	1 lb.	**1½ lb.**	**2 lb.**
water	¾ cup	1 cup	1⅛ cups
fresh cranberries	½ cup	¾ cup	1 cup
butter or vegetable oil	1½ tbs.	2½ tbs.	3 tbs.
honey	3 tbs.	¼ cup	⅓ cup
cornmeal	⅔ cup	¾ cup	1 cup
bread flour	2 cups	2½ cups	3 cups
rapid or quick yeast	1 tsp.	1½ tsp.	2 tsp.
flour equivalent	*2⅔ cups*	*3¼ cups*	*4 cups*
cycle	*white, sweet; no timer*		
setting	*light to medium*		

---

per 1 oz. 94 calories, 2.2 g protein, 17.7 g carbohydrate, 1.7 g fat, 0 mg cholesterol, 26 mg sodium

DATE BREAD

Dorothy requested an adaptation of a sugar-free quick bread using equal amounts of chopped dates and flour. That high amount of fruit would not work with a rapid or quick yeast product, so I came up with this flavorful yeast bread instead. I buy dates already chopped. Walnut meal is very finely ground walnuts. Let the dough knead for about 5 minutes before checking the consistency. Add a tablespoon of liquid if needed — I found slight variations using different dates.

	1 lb.	**1½ lb.**	**2 lb. *only***
water	⅔ cup	1 cup	1⅓ cups
apple juice concentrate	2 tbs.	3 tbs.	¼ cup
salt	½ tsp.	⅔ tsp.	¾ tsp.
chopped dates	¼ cup	⅓ cup	½ cup
walnut meal	½ cup	¾ cup	1 cup
bread flour	2 cups	3 cups	4 cups
rapid or quick yeast	1 tsp.	1½ tsp.	2 tsp.
flour equivalent	*2½ cups*	*3¾ cups*	*5 cups*
cycle	*sweet, white; no timer*		
setting	*light*		

per 1 oz.   83 calories, 2.8 g protein, 12.9 g carbohydrate, 2.5 g fat, 0 mg cholesterol, 67 mg sodium

66   FRUIT AND VEGETABLE BREADS

BLUEBERRY OATMEAL BREAD

LARRY JOCHIMS

Larry uses canned blueberries for this recipe (1 cup blueberries equals ½ a 15 oz. can). If using fresh blueberries, they should be mashed tightly into the measuring cup. As with any recipe using fruit for moisture, watch the dough and adjust with water or flour as needed.

	1 lb.	**1½ lb.**	**1¾ lb.**
blueberries and juice	1 cup	1¼ cups	1½ cups
canola oil	1 tbs.	1⅓ tbs.	1½ tbs.
sugar	1 tbs.	1⅓ tbs.	1½ tbs.
salt	¼ tsp.	⅓ tsp.	½ tsp.
oats	½ cup	¾ cup	1 cup
bread flour	2 cups	2½ cups	3 cups
rapid or quick yeast	1½ tsp.	2 tsp.	2 tsp.
flour equivalent	*2½ cups*	*3¼ cups*	*4 cups*
cycle	*white, sweet; no timer*		
setting	*light to medium*		

per 1 oz. *75 calories, 2.3 g protein, 13.7 g carbohydrate, 1.3 g fat, 0 mg cholesterol, 34 mg sodium*

CRANBERRY WALNUT BREAD

DORIE MEREDITH

Grind the walnuts in a food processor, or place nuts in a zip lock bag and roll with a rolling pin until coarsely ground. It's well worth the extra effort! Craisins are dried, sweetened cranberries. You can also use raisins or dried blueberries.

	1 lb.	1½ lb.	2 lb.
water	¾ cup	1⅛ cups	1½ cups
applesauce	2 tbs.	3 tbs.	¼ cup
canola oil	2½ tbs.	¼ cup	⅓ cup
sugar	1½ tbs.	2 tbs.	3 tbs.
salt	½ tsp.	¾ tsp.	1 tsp.
walnut meal	½ cup	¾ cup	1 cup
bread flour	2 cups	3 cups	4 cups
nonfat dry milk	1½ tbs.	2 tbs.	3 tbs.
rapid or quick yeast	1 tsp.	1½ tsp.	2 tsp.
*craisins	⅓ cup	½ cup	⅔ cup
flour equivalent	*2½ cups*	*3¾ cups*	*5 cups*
cycle	*white, sweet; timer*		
setting	*light to medium*		

*Add craisins at the beep or appropriate time for your machine.

per 1 oz. *109 calories, 3.0 g protein, 14.6 g carbohydrate, 4.6 g fat, 0 mg cholesterol, 70 mg sodium*

CRANBERRY BREAD

Kathy uses cranberry liqueur for a little additional cranberry flavor in this bread. You may use frozen cranberry juice concentrate (thawed) or combine the water and cranberry flavoring and use cranberry juice as a substitute if desired. Craisins are dried, sweetened cranberries.

	1 lb.	**1½ lb.**	**1¾ lb.**
water	⅔ cup	1 cup	1⅓ cups
cranberry flavoring	1½ tsp.	2 tsp.	1 tbs.
vegetable oil	1 tbs.	1½ tbs.	2 tbs.
honey	2 tbs.	3 tbs.	¼ cup
salt	⅓ tsp.	½ tsp.	⅔ tsp.
whole wheat flour	1 cup	1½ cups	2 cups
bread flour	1 cup	1½ cups	2 cups
rapid or quick yeast	1 tsp.	1½ tsp.	2 tsp.
*craisins	⅓ cup	½ cup	¾ cup
flour equivalent	*2 cups*	*3 cups*	*4 cups*
cycle	*white, sweet, wheat; timer*		
setting	*light to medium*		

*Add craisins at the beep or appropriate time for your machine.

per 1 oz. 76 calories, 2 g protein, 15.2 g carbohydrate, 1.1 g fat, 0 mg cholesterol, 50 mg sodium

ONION CHEESE BREAD

JOANNE MacGREGOR

Joanne says to add the cheese slowly as the machine is kneading. Watch the dough and adjust with water or flour as necessary. She adds it at the beep (raisin cycle) but it could also be added early during the second kneading cycle. If your machine stops kneading when the lid is open, add the cheese ¼ at a time, close lid until it is kneaded in and repeat until all cheese is added. The onion amounts are approximate and the flour should be adjusted to compensate for more or less liquid. Joanne actually uses 2 medium onions for the 1½ lb. size recipe — we found that provided much too much liquid for the dough. If the machine has difficulty kneading the ingredients into a dough ball, scrape the sides of the pan to help push the ingredients toward the kneading paddle.

	1 lb.	1½ lb.	1¾ lb.
diced onion	¼ cup	⅓ cup	½ cup
butter	1 tbs.	1 tbs.	1½ tbs.

Sauté diced medium onion in butter until soft. Set aside to cool. Place in the bread machine loaf pan and add the following ingredients:

milk	½ cup	¾ cup	1 cup
butter or margarine	1 tsp.	1½ tsp.	2 tsp.
sugar	1 tsp.	1½ tsp.	¾ tsp.
salt	¾ tsp.	1 tsp.	1 tsp.
bread flour	2 cups	3 cups	3½ cups
rapid or quick yeast	1 tsp.	1½ tsp.	2 tsp.
*grated cheddar	⅔ cup	1 cup	1¼ cups
flour equivalent	*2 cups*	*3 cups*	*3½ cups*
cycle	*white sweet; no timer*		
setting	*medium*		

*Add cheese during kneading.

---

per 1 oz.   *83 calories, 3.4 g protein, 11.2 g carbohydrate, 2.8 g fat, 7 mg cholesterol, 144 mg sodium*

PECAN RAISIN BREAD

NORMA McINTOSH

Norma uses Great Grains cereal with dates, raisins and pecans. This is a dense loaf.

	1 lb.	**1½ lb.**	**2 lb.**
water	¾ cup	1⅛ cups	1½ cups
butter or vegetable oil	1 tbs.	1½ tbs.	2 tbs.
honey	2 tbs.	3 tbs.	4 tbs.
salt	½ tsp.	¾ tsp.	1 tsp.
Great Grains cereal	⅓ cup	½ cup	⅔ cup
whole wheat flour	⅔ cup	1 cup	1⅓ cups
bread flour	1⅓ cups	2 cups	2⅔ cups
dry milk powder	1½ tbs.	2 tbs.	2½ tbs.
rapid or quick yeast	1 tsp.	1½ tsp.	2 tsp.
*raisins	3 tbs.	¼ cup	⅓ cup
*pecans, chopped	3 tbs.	¼ cup	⅓ cup
*oat bran	3 tbs.	¼ cup	⅓ cup
flour equivalent	*2⅓ cups*	*3½ cups*	*4⅔ cups*
cycle	*sweet, white; timer*		
setting	*light to medium*		

*Add at the beep or appropriate time for your machine.

---

per 1 oz.   101 calories, 4.5 g protein, 19 g carbohydrate, 2.2 g fat, 1 mg cholesterol, 109 mg sodium

MUSHROOM BREAD

ELIZABETH HAND

Elizabeth requested this adaptation of a favorite conventional recipe. She says the mushrooms "disappear" and give the bread lots of minerals and moisture. Use fresh mushrooms. Watch the dough carefully and adjust with water or flour as necessary.

	1 lb.	1½ lb.	1¾ lb.
water	¾ cup	1⅛ cups	1½ cups
mushrooms, finely chopped	2 tbs.	3 tbs.	¼ cup
vegetable oil	1½ tsp.	2 tsp.	1 tbs.
molasses	⅓ cup	½ cup	⅔ cup
salt	½ tsp.	¾ tsp.	1 tsp.
whole wheat flour	½ cup	¾ cup	1 cup
wheat germ	¼ cup	⅓ cup	½ cup
oats	¼ cup	⅓ cup	½ cup
bread flour	1½ cup	2⅓ cups	3 cups
rapid or quick yeast	1½ tsp.	2 tsp.	2½ tsp.
*raisins	¼ cup	⅓ cup	½ cup
flour equivalent	*2½ cups*	*3¾ cups*	*5 cups*
cycle	*wheat, sweet; timer*		
setting	*medium*		

*Add raisins at the beep or appropriate time for your machine.

per 1 oz.   *114 calories, 3.8 g protein, 22.1 g carbohydrate, 1.4 g fat, 0 mg cholesterol, 69 mg sodium*

APPLE CIDER BREAD

ELAINE BILLETS

Elaine came up with a delicious fall treat! If cider is not available, apple juice may be used. The sunflower seeds may be added at the beginning or at the beep. The 9 (or 7 or 12) grain cereal may be found in some large grocery stores or in health food stores.

	1 lb.	**1½ lb.**	**2 lb.**
apple cider	⅔ cup	1 cup	1⅓ cups
vegetable oil	1⅓ tbs.	2 tbs.	2⅔ tbs.
honey	1 tbs.	1½ tbs.	2 tbs.
salt	⅔ tsp.	1 tsp.	1 tsp.
9 grain cereal	⅔ cup	1 cup	1⅓ cups
bread flour	1⅓ cups	2 cups	2⅔ cups
sunflower seeds	¼ cup	⅓ cup	½ cup
rapid or quick yeast	1 tsp.	1½ tsp.	2 tsp.
flour equivalent	*2 cups*	*3 cups*	*4 cups*
cycle	*white, sweet; timer*		
setting	*medium*		

per 1 oz. 222 calories, 1.9 g protein, 11 g carbohydrate, 19.4 g fat, 0 mg cholesterol, 102 mg sodium

ORANGE CRAISIN BREAD

BARBARA MILLER

Barbara makes her own candied orange peel for this bread. Candied peel may be found in some gourmet shops or you may substitute regular fresh peel or 1/3 the amount with dried peel. The salt may be cut in half if desired. This is really good. Craisins are dried, sweetened cranberries.

	1 lb.	**1½ lb.**	**1¾ lb.**
water	1 cup	1⅓ cups	1½ cups
butter or margarine	1 tbs.	1⅓ tbs.	1½ tbs.
sugar	2 tbs.	3 tbs.	scant ¼ cup
salt	1 tsp.	1½ tsp.	1½ tsp.
candied orange peel	2 tbs.	3 tbs.	3½ tbs.
bread flour	2¼ cups	3 cups	3½ cups
powdered milk	1 tbs.	1½ tbs.	2 tbs.
rapid or quick yeast	1½ tsp.	2 tsp.	2 tsp.
*craisins	⅓ cup	½ cup	⅔ cup
flour equivalent	*2¼ cups*	*3 cups*	*3½ cups*
cycle	*sweet, white; timer*		
setting	*light*		

*Add craisins at the beep or appropriate time for your machine.

---

per 1 oz. *80 calories, 2.3 g protein, 15.7 g carbohydrate, 1 g fat, 0 mg cholesterol, 145 mg sodium*

SAUERKRAUT RYE

JEAN SCHENK

Jean requested a recipe for a bread which she purchased in the past. With only a name to go on, I hope this compares favorably! I did not add caraway seeds but they could be added to taste. The instant coffee gives the bread its dark color.

	1 lb.	**1½ lb.**	**2 lb.**
water	⅔ cup	1 cup	1⅓ cups
vegetable oil	1 tbs.	1½ tbs.	2 tbs.
molasses	2 tbs.	3 tbs.	¼ cup
sauerkraut	¼ cup	⅓ cup	½ cup
salt	½ tsp.	¾ tsp.	1 tsp.
instant coffee granules	1 tbs.	1½ tbs.	2 tbs.
rye flour	½ cup	¾ cup	1 cup
bread flour	1¾ cups	2½ cups	3½ cups
vital gluten	1 tbs.	1½ tbs.	2 tbs.
rapid or quick yeast	1½ tsp.	2 tsp.	2¼ tsp.
flour equivalent	*2¼ cups*	*3¼ cups*	*4½ cups*
cycle	*wheat, white; no timer*		
setting	*medium*		

per 1 oz. 72calories, 2.4 g protein, 13.3 g carbohydrate, 1.2 g fat, 0 mg cholesterol, 92 mg sodium

TOMATO BREAD

This is an adaptation of a favorite recipe of Ramona's. If using commercially prepared canned tomato juice, omit the salt. Seasonings may be adjusted to taste.

	1 lb.	**1½ lb.**	**1¾ lb.**
tomato juice	¾ cup	1⅛ cups	1⅓ cups
vegetable oil	1 tbs.	1 tbs.	1½ tbs.
salt	½ tsp.	¾ tsp.	1 tsp.
sugar	2 tbs.	3 tbs.	¼ cup
ground ginger	pinch	dash	¼ tsp.
celery seed	1½ tsp.	2 tsp.	2½ tsp.
Italian seasoning	¼ tsp.	⅓ tsp.	½ tsp.
bread flour	2 cups	3 cups	3½ cups
rapid or quick yeast	1½ tsp.	2 tsp.	2 tsp.
flour equivalent	*2 cups*	*3 cups*	*3½ cups*
cycle	*white; timer*		
setting	*medium*		

---

per 1 oz. *67 calories, 2.0 g protein, 12.3 g carbohydrate,. 1.1 g fat, 0 mg cholesterol, 109 mg sodium*

FRUIT AND VEGETABLE BREADS 77

TROPICAL BANANA CHIP BREAD

LAURIE COFFINO

Laurie says she finds the high amount of gluten is necessary in this moist, tropical bread. It should rise to a medium height with the gluten because of the high amount of sugar. As with any bread which uses a fruit for all or part of the liquid, watch the dough carefully. If you elect to use a medium-sized banana and not measure it precisely, take care to watch the dough. Add water or flour as necessary, one tablespoon at a time. Use very ripe bananas. The banana chips should be crushed. Pineapple extract may be used in place of the coconut if desired.

	1 lb.	**1½ lb.**	**1¾ lb.**
orange juice	⅓ cup	½ cup	⅔ cup
mashed bananas	⅞ cup	1¼ cups	1½ cups
vegetable oil	1⅓ tbs.	2 tbs.	2 tbs.
honey	3 tbs.	¼ cup	¼ cup
coconut extract	1½ tsp.	2 tsp.	2½ tsp.
salt	⅔ tsp.	1 tsp.	1 tsp.
orange peel	⅔ tsp.	1 tsp.	1 tsp.
coconut flakes	⅔ cup	1 cup	1¼ cups
bread flour	2 cups	3 cups	3½ cups

vital gluten	1/4 cup	1/3 cup	1/3 cup
rapid or quick yeast	1 1/2 tsp.	2 tsp.	2 tsp.
*banana chips	1/2 cup	3/4 cup	3/4+ cup
flour equivalent	*2 3/4 cups*	*4 cups*	*5 cups*
cycle	*sweet, white; no timer*		
setting	*light*		

*Add banana chips at the beep or appropriate time for your machine.

per 1 oz. *126 calories, 4.2 g protein, 21.3 g carbohydrate, 3 g fat, 0 mg cholesterol, 100 mg sodium*

BANANA RAISIN NUT BREAD

JANIS BOSENKO

Janis says that this bread is such a big hit with friends and co-workers that she has regular customers who order loaves for purchase! It also won her a blue ribbon from the "Machine Made Bread" category at the Marin County Fair. The banana should be very ripe, medium in size, and cut into chunks. Bananas vary in moisture content, so adjust the water or flour as necessary, 1 tablespoon at a time. Use either a yolk or white for the half egg. The cinnamon may be adjusted to taste. This is a low-rising, moist loaf of bread with great taste and texture. If you are a chocoholic like me, substitute all or half of the raisins with chocolate chips — Mmmmm! If your machine is prone to the doughy blues, cut the raisins and nuts in half.

	1 lb.	1½ lb.	1¾ + lb.
water	⅓ cup	½ cup	⅔ cup
egg	½	½	1
vegetable oil	1 tbs.	1½ tbs.	2 tbs.
honey	2 tbs.	3 tbs.	¼ cup
banana	¾	1	1½
salt	½ tsp.	¾ tsp.	1 tsp.
cinnamon	½ tsp.	¾ tsp.	1 tsp.

bread flour	2 cups	3 cups	3½ cups
rapid or quick yeast	1 tsp.	1½ tsp.	2 tsp.
*raisins	½ cup	¾ cup	1 cup
*broken walnuts	¼ cup	⅓ cup	½ cup
flour equivalent	*2 cups*	*3 cups*	*3½ cups*
cycle	*white, sweet; raisin*		
setting	*light to medium*		

*Add raisins and nuts at the beep or appropriate time for your machine.

per 1 oz. *95 calories, 2.6 g protein, 17 g carbohydrate, 2.3 g fat, 0 mg cholesterol, 69 mg sodium*

APRICOT ALMOND BREAD

CAROL ASHMAN

Carol Ashman uses "slab" apricots for this recipe as they are the sweetest she has found. I tested using dried apricots from a grocery store. She says the real trick to this bread is to mix the additional ingredients together so that the sugar coats the almonds and apricots. All additional ingredients should be well chopped. Add them at the appropriate time for your machine. This is a "must try." If your machine is prone to the doughy blues, cut the fruit and nut amounts in half and cover the glass <u>only</u> with a small piece of aluminum foil, but don't block the air vents. I buy almond paste in the grocery store in a 7 oz. roll and use ½ of the roll to equal about ⅔ cup diced and slightly less for the ½ cup and slightly more for the ¾ cup.

	1 lb.	1½ lb.	1¾ lb.
water	⅔ cup	1 cup	1 cup
egg	1	1½	2
almond extract	1 tsp.	1½ tsp.	2 tsp.
vegetable oil	2 tbs.	3 tbs.	¼ cup
salt	¼ tsp.	⅓ tsp.	½ tsp.
sugar	¼ cup	⅓ cup	⅓ cup
bread flour	2 cups	3 cups	3½ cups

rapid or quick yeast	1½ tsp.	1½ tsp.	2 tsp.
*almonds, chopped	¼ cup	⅓ cup	½ cup
*dried apricots, diced	½ cup	¾ cup	1 cup
*almond paste, diced	½ cup	⅔ cup	⅔ cup
*sugar	2 tbs.	3 tbs.	¼ cup
flour equivalent	*2 cups*	*3 cups*	*3½ cups*
cycle	*white, sweet; no timer*		
setting	*light*		

*Add at the beep or appropriate time for your machine.

---

per 1 oz. *135 calories, 3.5 g protein, 19.4 g carbohydrate, 3.4 g fat, 0 mg cholesterol, 38 mg sodium*

CHERRY ALMOND BREAD

Larane loves cherries and couldn't find a recipe using them so she made one up. She uses the gluten to obtain a tall, moist loaf which has a slightly tart cherry flavor. Larane packs cherries tightly in the measuring cup. She uses twice the amount of yeast — I do not find that much necessary. This is a low rising, dense loaf.

	1 lb.	**1½ lb.**	**1¾ lb.**
canned tart cherries	1 cup	1½ cups	1¾ cups
almond extract	¾ tsp.	1 tsp.	1 tsp.
butter	1½ tbs.	2 tbs.	2½ tbs.
salt	¾ tsp.	1 tsp.	1 tsp.
sugar	¼ cup	⅓ cup	½ cup
bread flour	2 cups	3 cups	3½ cups
vital gluten	1½ tbs.	2 tbs.	2½ tbs.
rapid or quick yeast	1 tsp.	1½ tsp.	2 tsp.
*slivered almonds	⅓ cup	½ cup	⅔ cup
flour equivalent	*2 cups*	*3 cups*	*3½ cups*
cycle	*sweet, white; no timer*		
setting	*light*		

*Add cherries at the beep or appropriate time for your machine.

per 1 oz. *105 calories, 2.9 g protein, 17.5 g carbohydrate, 2.9 g fat, 0 mg cholesterol, 115 mg sodium*

84   FRUIT AND VEGETABLE BREADS

BING CHERRY COCONUT BREAD

TRISH BOYER

Trish says to make sure to use coconut milk, not cream of coconut.

	1 lb.	**1½ lb.**	**2 lb.**
coconut milk	⅔ cup	1 cup	1⅓ cups
walnut or vegetable oil	1½ tbs.	2⅓ tbs.	3 tbs.
honey	1½ tbs.	2⅓ tbs.	3 tbs.
egg	½	½	1
salt	⅓ tsp.	½ tsp.	¾ tsp.
whole wheat flour	½ cup	¾ cup	1 cup
rolled oats	½ cup	¾ cup	1 cup
bread flour	1 cup	1½ cups	2 cups
rapid or quick yeast	1 tsp.	1½ tsp.	2 tsp.
*dried Bing cherries	¼ cup	⅓ cup	½ cup
*flaked coconut	¼ cup	⅓ cup	½ cup
*sliced almonds	2 tbs.	3 tbs.	¼ cup
flour equivalent	*2 cups*	*3 cups*	*4 cups*
cycle	*sweet, white; no timer*		
setting	*light to medium*		

*Add at the beep or appropriate time for your machine.

---

per 1 oz. *96 calories, 2.4 g protein, 12.5 g carbohydrate, 4.4 g fat, 0 mg cholesterol, 51 mg sodium*

SWEET POTATO BREAD

LILLIAN HO

Lillian says that the sweet potato adds a wonderful, moist texture and subtle taste to this bread. Cook and place the approximate amount of sweet potato into a 2-cup measuring cup, add the egg and fill with water up to the given measurement mark. The machine will mash the sweet potato for you. This is a very high rising bread which is great for turkey sandwiches.

	1 lb.	**1½ lb.**	**2 lb.**
sweet potato, cooked (or yam)	⅔ cup	¾ cup	1 cup
egg	1	1	1
water	as needed	as needed	as needed
wet ingredients should equal	1 cup	1½ cups	2 cups
butter	1½ tbs.	2 tbs.	2½ tbs.
brown sugar	1½ tbs.	2 tbs.	2½ tbs.
salt	¾ tsp.	1 tsp.	1 tsp.
cinnamon	⅓ tsp.	½ tsp.	⅔ tsp.
nutmeg	¼ tsp.	⅓ tsp.	½ tsp.
allspice	¼ tsp.	⅓ tsp.	½ tsp.
whole wheat flour	⅓ cup	½ cup	⅔ cup

| bread flour | 1⅔ cups | 2½ cups | 3⅓ cups |
| rapid or quick yeast | 1 tsp. | 1½ tsp. | 2 tsp. |

flour equivalent	*2 cups*	*3 cups*	*4 cups*
cycle	*white, sweet; no timer*		
setting	*medium*		

per 1 oz.   *78 calories, 2.4 g protein, 13.4 g carbohydrate, 1.7 g fat, 13 mg cholesterol, 125 mg sodium*

LAZY ONION BREAD

WENDY CERACCHE

The lazy part of this recipe is simply using onion soup mix! Thanks to Wendy for sharing this one. There is no salt included in the recipe as there is some in the onion soup.

	1 lb.	1½ lb.	1¾ lb.
water or milk	7/8 cup (7 oz.)	1¼ cups	1½ cups
sugar	1½ tbs.	2 tbs.	2½ tbs.
onion soup mix	1½ tsp.	2 tsp.	1 tbs.
bread flour	2 cups	3 cups	3½ cups
dry milk powder, optional	1 tbs.	1 tbs.	1½ tbs.
rapid or quick yeast	1 tsp.	1½ tsp.	2 tsp.
flour equivalent	*2 cups*	*3 cups*	*3½ cups*
cycle	*white; timer*		
setting	*medium*		

---

per 1 oz. *57 calories, 2.0 g protein, 11.5 g carbohydrate,. .4 g fat, 0 mg cholesterol, 31 mg sodium*

COCONUT BREAD

BEAULAH DONISON

Beulah says her family frequently requests this bread. Be sure to use unsweetened coconut milk such as A Taste of Thai, not the cream of coconut milk. Use an egg yolk, white or 2 tbs. egg substitute for the half egg.

	1 lb.	**1½ lb.**	**2 lb. *only***
coconut milk	⅔ cup	1 cup	1¼ cups
egg	½	½	1
vegetable oil	1 tbs.	1½ tbs.	2 tbs.
coconut extract	1 tsp.	1½ tsp.	1 tsp.
sugar	2 tbs.	2½ tbs.	3 tbs.
salt	½ tsp.	¾ tsp.	1 tsp.
coconut flakes	¼ cup	⅓ cup	½ cup
bread flour	2 cups	3 cups	3¾ cups
yeast	1 tsp.	1½ tsp.	2 tsp.
flour equivalent	*2¼ cups*	*3⅓ cups*	*4¼ cups*
cycle setting:	*sweet, white; no timer missing*		

per 1 oz. 89 calories, 2.2 g protein, 12.6 g carbohydrate, 3.5 g fat, 0 mg cholesterol, 73 mg sodium

CZECHOSLOVAKIAN ORANGE BREAD

Ruth requested this recipe adaptation. This bread is traditionally baked in a crescent and is glazed with honey and orange juice mixed together and warmed.

	1 lb.	**1½ lb.**	**1¾ lb.**
milk	½ cup	⅔ cup	¾ cup
butter or margarine	3 tbs.	4 tbs.	5 tbs.
egg	1	1	1
salt	¼ tsp.	⅓ tsp.	½ tsp.
sugar	3 tbs.	¼ cup	⅓ cup
orange peel	1 tsp.	1 ¼ tsp.	1½ tsp.
ground mace	dash	¼ tsp.	¼ tsp.
bread flour	2 cups	3 cups	3½ cups
rapid or quick yeast	1 tsp.	1 tsp.	1½ tsp.
flour equivalent	*2 cups*	*3 cups*	*3½ cups*
cycle	*sweet, white; no timer*		
setting	*light*		

per 1 oz. *84 calories, 2.5 g protein, 12.9 g carbohydrate, 2.7 g fat, 1 mg cholesterol, 69 mg sodium*

90 FRUIT AND VEGETABLE BREADS

HERB BREADS

Herbs and spices may be adjusted to taste without affecting the texture of the loaf. In general, if using fresh herbs, triple the amount listed for dried herbs.

GARLIC DILL WHOLE WHEAT BREAD   VIRGINIA COLSON

Virginia makes this flavorful bread for family and friends. Celery seed or rosemary may be substituted for the dill weed. Use 3 or 4 cloves of minced or pressed garlic for every teaspoon of powder if desired.

	1 lb.	1½ lb.	1¾ lb.
water	⅞ cup (7 oz.)	1¼ cups	1¾ cups
butter or margarine	1 tbs.	1½ tbs.	2 tbs.
salt	½ tsp.	¾ tsp.	1 tsp.
garlic powder	1 tsp.	1½ tsp.	2 tsp.
dill weed	2 tsp.	1 tbs.	1⅓ tbs.
bread flour	1 cup	1½ cups	2 cups
whole wheat flour	1 cup	1½ cups	2 cups
nonfat dry milk	1 tbs.	1½ tbs.	2 tbs.
rapid or quick yeast	1½ tsp.	2 tsp.	2 tsp.
flour equivalent	*2 cups*	*3 cups*	*4 cups*
cycle	*white, wheat; timer*		
setting	*medium*		

---

per 1 oz.   *59 calories, 2.1 g protein, 10.9 g carbohydrate, 1 g fat, mg cholesterol, 79 mg sodium*

GARLIC-DILL BREAD

LYNN CONNOR

Lynn uses the bottled chopped or crushed garlic (salt free) for this garlic bread. The garlic and dill combine nicely. This low to medium rising bread has a good, dense texture and is very garlicky!

	1 lb.	**1½ lb.**	**2 lb.**
water	⅔ cup	1 cup	1⅓ cups
chopped garlic	¼ cup	⅓ cup	½ cup
butter	1 tbs.	1½ tbs.	2 tbs.
dill weed or seed	½ tsp.	¾ tsp.	1 tsp.
salt	½ tsp.	¾ tsp.	1 tsp.
bread flour	1⅛ cups	1⅔ cups	2¼ cups
whole wheat flour	1⅛ cups	1⅔ cups	2¼ cups
rapid or quick yeast	1 tsp.	1½ tsp.	2 tsp.
flour equivalent	*2¼ cups*	*3⅓ cups*	*4½ cups*
cycle	*wheat, sweet, white; timer*		
setting	*light*		

---

per 1 oz. *69 calories, 2.5 g protein, 13.2 g carbohydrate, 1 g fat, 0 mg cholesterol, 78 mg sodium*

ZAHTAR BREAD

KAREN ABU-HAMDEH

Karen says this bread is wonderful and I agree. If you do not have zahtar, oregano or thyme may be substituted. Zahtar is a Middle Eastern spice blend and is available through mail order sources (see page 166).

	1 lb.	1½ lb.	1¾ lb.
water	¾ cup	1⅛ cups	1⅓ cups
olive oil	1½ tbs.	2 tbs.	2½ tbs.
sugar	¾ tsp.	1 tsp.	1¼ tsp.
salt	¾ tsp.	1 tsp.	1 tsp.
zahtar	1½ tbs.	2 tbs.	2½ tbs.
bread flour	2 cups	3 cups	3½ cups
rapid or quick yeast	1 tsp.	1½ tsp.	2 tsp.
flour equivalent	*2 cups*	*3 cups*	*3½ cups*
cycle	*white, French, sweet; timer*		
setting	*medium*		

per 1 oz. *63 calories, 1.8 g protein, 10.5 g carbohydrate, 1.5 g fat, 0 mg cholesterol, 100 mg sodium*

INDIAN YOGURT BREAD

PRISCILLA WARD

Priscilla has fun developing recipes for use in her Maxim machine. Garam masala is a blend of Indian spices and may be found in Indian and Asian grocery stores. Any spice blend may be substituted. Add milk slowly after the machine has been kneading for 3 to 4 minutes. Use only enough for the dough to form a round ball.

	1 lb.	**1½ lb.**	**2 lb.**
plain yogurt	1 cup	1½ cups	1¾ cups
olive oil	2 tbs.	3 tbs.	¼ cup
honey	2 tbs.	3 tbs.	¼ cup
garam masala	1 tsp.	1½ tsp.	2 tsp.
salt	½ tsp.	¾ tsp.	1 tsp.
bread flour	2 cup	3 cups	3½ cups
whole wheat flour	¾ cup	1⅛ cups	1⅓ cups
rapid or quick yeast	1½ tsp.	2 tsp.	2½ tsp.
*milk	as needed; add 1-2 tbs. at a time		
flour equivalent	*2¾ cups*	*4⅛ cups*	*4¾ cups*
cycle	*wheat, white, sweet; no timer*		
setting	*light*		

per 1 oz.   102 calories, 3.4 g protein, 17.6 g carbohydrate, 2.3 g fat, 1 mg cholesterol, 77 mg sodium

ITALIAN HERB BREAD

MRS. WILLIAM MILLER

Mrs. Miller says this recipe is "growling good" and serves it with spaghetti. Use freshly grated Parmesan cheese.

	1 lb.	1½ lb.	1¾ lb.
water	¾ cup	1⅛ cups	1⅓ cups
olive oil	2 tsp.	1 tbs.	1⅓ tbs.
sugar	2 tsp.	1 tbs.	1⅓ tbs.
Parmesan cheese, grated	¼ cup	⅓ cup	½ cup
garlic powder	½ tsp.	1 tsp.	1 tsp.
Italian seasoning	½ tsp.	1 tsp.	1 tsp.
bread flour	2 cups	3 cups	3½ cups
rapid or quick yeast	1 tsp.	1½ tsp.	2 tsp.
flour equivalent	*2 cups*	*3 cups*	*3½ cups*
cycle	*white, French; timer*		
setting	*medium*		

---

per 1 oz. *65 calories, 2.5 g protein, 10.9 g carbohydrate, 1.2 g fat, 1 mg cholesterol, 31 mg sodium*

SAVORY HERB CORN BREAD

BETH DASH KORUITZ

Beth uses defatted chicken broth. Chicken bouillon may be substituted. She serves this warm with a garlic butter spread or in poultry dressing.

	1 lb.	**1½ lb.**	**2 lb.**
chicken broth	½ cup	¾ cup	1 cup
water	⅓ cup	½ cup	⅔ cup
canola oil	2 tbs.	1 tbs.	1⅓ tbs.
molasses	1 tbs.	1 ½ tbs.	2 tbs.
salt	¾ tsp.	1 tsp.	1 tsp.
sage	1 tsp.	1½ tsp.	2 tsp.
cornmeal	¼ cup	⅓ cup	½ cup
instant potato flakes	¼ cup	⅓ cup	½ cup
bread flour	1¾ cup	2⅔ cups	3½ cups
milk powder	1 tbs.	1½ tbs.	2 tbs.
rapid or quick yeast	1 tsp.	1½ tsp.	2 tsp.
flour equivalent	*2¼ cups*	*3⅓ cups*	*4½ cups*
cycle	*white; timer*		
setting	*medium*		

per 1 oz.   67 calories, 1.9 g protein, 10.5 g carbohydrate, 1.98 g fat, 0 mg cholesterol, 127 mg sodium

NORMA'S DILLY BREAD

NORMA HERBERT

Norma's aunt gave her this recipe years ago and Norma requested an adaptation for her bread machine. She recommends using creamed cottage cheese. The minced instant onion is found with spices in your grocery store. The cottage cheese can throw off the liquid balance — adjust with water or flour 1 tablespoon at a time.

	1 lb.	1½ lb.	1¾ lb.
cottage cheese	¾ cup	1 cup	1⅛ cups
egg	1	2	2
sugar	1½ tbs.	2 tbs.	3 tbs.
salt	½ tsp.	1 tsp.	1 tsp.
onion or onion powder	2 tsp.	1 tbs.	1⅓ tbs.
baking soda	¼ tsp.	½ tsp.	½ tsp.
dill seed	1½ tsp.	2 tsp.	1 tbs.
bread flour	2 cups	3 cups	3½ cups
rapid or quick yeast	1 tsp.	1½ tsp.	2 tsp.
flour equivalent	*2 cups*	*3 cups*	*3½ cups*
cycle	*white, sweet; no timer*		
setting	*light to medium*		

per 1 oz. 69 calories, 3.7 g protein, 11.9 g carbohydrate, 0.8 g fat, 10 mg cholesterol, 126 mg sodium

HERB BREAD

MARIE EHLERS

Marie recently bought a bread machine and has already adapted this recipe. The green onions may throw off the moisture content slightly, so watch the dough and adjust with flour or water if needed. I cut her salt amount in half.

	1 lb.	1½ lb.	2 lb.
water	⅞ cup (7 oz.)	1¼ cups	1½ cups
vegetable oil	1 tbs.	1⅓ tbs.	1½ tbs.
salt	½ tsp.	¾ tsp.	1 tsp.
sugar	1 tbs.	1⅓ tbs.	1½ tbs.
green onion tops, chopped	3 tbs.	¼ cup	⅓ cup
fresh parsley, chopped	2 tbs.	2½ tbs.	3 tbs.
or dried parsley	1 tsp.	1¼ tsp.	1½ tsp.
dill seed	1 tsp.	1¼ tsp.	1½ tsp.
caraway seed	1 tsp.	1¼ tsp.	1½ tsp.
bread flour	2⅛ cups	3 cups	3¾ cups
rapid or quick yeast	1 tsp.	1½ tsp.	2 tsp.
flour equivalent	*2⅛ cups*	*3 cups*	*3¾ cups*
cycle	*white; timer*		
setting	*medium*		

per 1 oz. 66 calories, 2.1 g protein, 12 g carbohydrate, 1.1 g fat, 0 mg cholesterol, 68 mg sodium

GARLIC HERB CHEESE BREAD

Camille made this "BBM" (before bread machine) and adapted it to fit her machine. She recommends using sharp cheddar as it gives the bread more flavor. Some people have said that they have difficulty with breads using garlic — that they don't rise. We have never experienced this in the test kitchen. All of our test loaves on this recipe rose very high. Keep an eye on the dough and adjust as necessary because of the cheese. The cheese should be lightly packed in the measuring cup. The garlic and herbs may be adjusted to taste. Scrape the sides of the pan with a rubber spatula if the ingredients are not mixing.

	1 lb.	1½ lb.	1¾ lb.
milk	½ cup	⅝ cup (5 oz.)	¾ cup
eggs	2	2	3
butter or margarine	2 tbs.	2½ tbs.	3 tbs.
grated cheese, lightly packed	¾ cup	1 cup	1 cup
salt	½ tsp.	1 tsp.	1 tsp.
sugar	1½ tsp.	2 tsp.	2½ tsp.
garlic clove, minced	1	1½	1½
cayenne pepper	dash	⅛ tsp.	¼ tsp.

oregano, dried	1/8+ tsp.	1/4 tsp.	1/3 tsp.
basil, dried	1/4 tsp.	1/2 tsp.	1/2 tsp.
caraway seeds	1 1/2 tsp.	2 tsp.	2 1/2 tsp.
bread flour	2 cups	3 cups	3 1/2 cups
rapid or quick yeast	1 tsp.	1 1/2 tsp.	2 tsp.
flour equivalent	*2 cups*	*3 cups*	*3 1/2 cups*
cycle	*white, sweet; no timer*		
setting	*light to medium*		

per 1 oz. *93 calories, 3.9 g protein, 11.3 g carbohydrate, 3.6 g fat, 6 mg cholesterol, 129 mg sodium*

OREGANO HERB BREAD

ROMAINE BLOUNT

Romaine came up with this bread for her husband. If using fresh herbs, triple the amount. Leftovers, if there are any, make flavorful croutons.

	1 lb.	**1½ lb.**	**1¾ lb.**
water	1 cup	1½ cups	1⅔ cups
olive oil	2 tbs.	3 tbs.	3 tbs.
sugar	⅓ tsp.	½ tsp.	⅔ tsp.
salt	½ tsp.	¾ tsp.	¾ tsp.
parsley	1 tsp.	1½ tsp.	1¾ tsp.
thyme, dried	1 tsp.	1½ tsp.	1¾ tsp.
oregano, dried	2 tsp.	1 tbs.	1⅓ tbs.
bread flour	2¼ cups	3 cups	3½ cups
dry milk	3 tbs.	¼ cup	⅓ cup
rapid or quick yeast	1½ tsp.	2 tsp.	2 tsp.
flour equivalent	*2¼ cups*	*3 cups*	*3½ cups*
cycle	*white; timer*		
setting	*medium*		

per 1 oz.   *76 calories, 2.4 g protein, 12.2 g carbohydrate, 2 g fat, 0 mg cholesterol, 72 mg sodium*

DILL ONION BREAD

FLARANE WOLD

Flarane enjoys making this bread with sour cream, but yogurt could also be used. Keep an eye on the dough and adjust the consistency with flour or water as necessary. Use an egg yolk, white or 2 tbs. egg substitute for the half egg.

	1 lb.	**1½ lb.**	**1¾ lb.**
sour cream	1 cup	1½ cups	1¾ cups
egg	1	1	1½
salt	½ tsp.	1 tsp.	1 tsp.
baking soda	¼ tsp.	⅓ tsp.	½ tsp.
sugar	2 tbs.	3 tbs.	¼ cup
dried onion flakes	2 tbs.	3 tbs.	3 tbs.
dill weed	1 tbs.	1⅓ tbs.	1½ tbs.
bread flour	2 cups	3 cups	3½ cups
rapid or quick yeast	1 tsp.	1½ tsp.	1½ tsp.
flour equivalent	*2 cups*	*3 cups*	*3½ cups*
cycle	*white, sweet; no timer*		
setting	*medium*		

per 1 oz. *90 calories, 2.6 g protein, 12.8 g carbohydrate, 3.3 g fat, 6 mg cholesterol, 91 mg sodium*

FRENCH HERB BREAD

KAREN SWANSON

Karen based this recipe on a bread that was a grand champion winner at the Alaska State Fair a few years ago. Karen normally likes to make whole grain breads but uses white flour for this as the flavors of the herbs carry better. If using the "green can" Parmesan cheese, omit the salt. Use an egg yolk, white or 2 tbs. egg substitute for the half egg. If using fresh herbs, triple the amount given. Herbs may be adjusted to taste.

	1 lb.	1½ lb.	1¾ lb.
water	⅔ cup	⅞ cup (7 oz.)	1 cup
vegetable oil	½ tbs.	1 tbs.	1 tbs.
egg	½	1	1
salt, optional	½ tsp.	¾ tsp.	1 tsp.
sugar	2½ tsp.	1 tbs.	1⅓ tbs.
garlic powder	dash	⅛ tsp.	¼ tsp.
Italian seasoning	dash	⅛ tsp.	¼ tsp.
oregano, dried	¼ tsp.	⅓ tsp.	½ tsp.
basil, dried	¼ tsp.	⅓ tsp.	½ tsp.
thyme, dried	¼ tsp.	⅓ tsp.	½ tsp.

Parmesan cheese, grated	2 tsp.	1 tbs.	1$\frac{1}{3}$ tbs.
bread flour	2$\frac{1}{4}$ cups	3 cups	3$\frac{1}{2}$ cups
dry milk powder	2 tbs.	2$\frac{1}{2}$ tbs.	3 tbs.
rapid or quick yeast	1 tsp.	1$\frac{1}{2}$ tsp.	2 tsp.
flour equivalent	*2$\frac{1}{4}$ cups*	*3 cups*	*3$\frac{1}{2}$ cups*
cycle	*white, French, no timer*		
setting	*medium*		

per 1 oz. *67 calories, 2.4 g protein, 12.5 g carbohydrate, 0.8 g fat, 0 mg cholesterol, 97 mg sodium*

SUGAR FREE ITALIAN HERB BREAD
ALBERT SANTONI

Albert Santoni cannot eat sugar or any other sweeteners so he came up with this sweetener-free bread. He suggests substituting rosemary, garlic powder and/or dill for the oregano. He says that that after one day, this bread makes a delicious appetizer toasted with extra virgin olive oil drizzled on top and a little salt and pepper. Herbs may be adjusted to taste and the amount should be tripled if using fresh herbs.

	1 lb.	1½ lb.	1¾ lb.
water	⅔ cup	1 cup	1¼ cups
olive oil	1⅓ tbs.	2 tbs.	2½ tbs.
salt	⅓ tsp.	½ tsp.	½ tsp.
oregano, dried	1 tsp.	1½ tsp.	2 tsp.
bread flour	2 cups	3 cups	3½ cups
rapid or quick yeast	1 tsp.	1½ tsp.	1½ tsp.
flour equivalent	*2 cups*	*3 cups*	*3½ cups*
cycle	*white, French - no fast cycle; timer*		
setting	*medium*		

per 1 oz. *61 calories, 1.9 g protein, 10.3 g carbohydrate, 1.4 g fat, 0 mg cholesterol, 45 mg sodium*

ONION SOUP BREAD

EVELYN FEHRMANN

Evelyn and a friend make this in their bread machines. The (Lipton's) onion soup mix may be adjusted to taste. After 10 minutes of kneading, adjust the consistency of the dough as needed by adding a tablespoon of water at a time until a dough ball is formed — it may require none, or up to 4 tbs. depending on the loaf size.

	1 lb.	1½ lb.	1¾ lb.
cottage cheese	½ cup	⅔ cup	¾ cup
sour cream	½ cup	⅔ cup	¾ cup
egg	½	1	1
butter or margarine	1 tbs.	1 tbs.	1½ tbs.
sugar	2 tbs.	2½ tbs.	3 tbs.
baking soda	¼ tsp.	¼ tsp.	½ tsp.
onion soup mix	2 tbs.	1½ tbs.	3 tbs.
bread flour	2¼ cups	3 cups	3½ cups
rapid or quick yeast	1 tsp.	1 tsp.	1½ tsp.
flour equivalent	*2¼ cups*	*3 cups*	*3½ cups*
cycle	*no timer*		
setting	*medium*		

per 1 oz. 93 calories, 3.5 g protein, 13.6 g carbohydrate, 2.8 g fat, 4 mg cholesterol, 120 mg sodium

PIZZA BREAD

Chris says this bread has a marvelous pizza taste and aroma with an earthy color. Her grandchildren love this so much there is frequently none left for the grownups!

	1 lb.	**1½ lb.**	**1¾ lb.**
tomato or V-8 juice	⅞ cup (7 oz.)	1¼ cups	1⅓ cups
vegetable oil	1½ tbs.	2 tbs.	2½ tbs.
egg (egg yolk or white for ½)	½	½	1
Parmesan cheese, freshly grated	3 tbs.	¼ cup	⅓ cup
basil, dried	2 tsp.	1 tbs.	1 tbs.
oregano, dried	⅓ tsp.	½ tsp.	¾ tsp.
sugar	1½ tbs.	2 tbs.	2 tbs.
salt	½ tsp.	1 tsp.	1 tsp.
garlic powder	½ tsp.	1 tsp.	1 tsp.
onion powder	½ tsp.	1 tsp.	1 tsp.
bread flour	2 cups	3 cups	3½ cups
rapid or quick yeast	1 tsp.	1½ tsp.	1½ tsp.
flour equivalent	*2 cups*	*3 cups*	*3½ cups*
cycle	*white, sweet; no timer*		
setting	*light*		

per 1 oz.   79 calories, 2.6 g protein, 12.2 g carbohydrate, 2.2 g fat, 14 mg cholesterol, 134 mg sodium

GOOD SEASONS BREAD

Lee makes this on his quick/rapid cycle (we tested on the basic white cycles) and uses Good Seasons Garlic Cheese Salad Dressing mix. We tested using several different brands and found that we preferred either a Good Seasons blend or a Mrs. Dash Dressing Mix (jar). If the dry seasoning mixes contain salt, none needs to be added to the bread. One .65 oz. package of mix equals about 2½ tbs. and may be used for all sizes. I cut Lee's water amount to avoid overflows. The water amount is less for the 1¾ lb. size because of the amount of eggs.

	1 lb.	**1½ lb.**	**1¾ lb.**
water	½ cup	¾ cups	⅔ cups
egg	1	1	2
canola oil	1½ tbs.	2 tbs.	2 tbs.
salt, optional	¼ tsp.	½ tsp.	½ tsp.
sugar	1 tbs.	1½ tbs.	1½ tbs.
salad dressing mix	2½ tbs.	2½ tbs.	2½ tbs.
bread flour	2 cups	3 cups	3½ cups
rapid or quick yeast	1 tsp.	1½ tsp.	2 tsp.
flour equivalent	*2 cups*	*3 cups*	*3½ cups*
cycle	white, no timer		
setting	medium		

per 1 oz.   *67 calories, 2.1 g protein, 11 g carbohydrate,. 1.5 g fat, 0 mg cholesterol, 37 mg sodium*

VEGETABLE HERB BREAD

CAMILLE CARTER

Camille says she hopes others enjoy this recipe as much as her family. It is a wonderful, spicy light-textured and colored bread which she calls "Old-Fashioned Stuffing Bread" and uses for leftover turkey sandwiches. Watch dough for moisture.

	1 lb.	1½ lb.	1¾ lb.
water	¾ cup	1⅛ cups	1⅓ cups
butter or margarine	½ tbs.	1 tbs.	1 tbs.
diced onion	¼ cup	⅓ cup	⅓ cup
sugar	1 tsp.	1½ tsp.	2 tsp.
salt	¾ tsp.	1 tsp.	1 tsp.
black pepper	¾ tsp.	1 tsp.	1 tsp.
sage	¾ tsp.	1 tsp.	1 tsp.
thyme, dried	1½ tsp.	2 tsp.	2 tsp.
diced celery including leafy top	¼ cup	⅓ cup	½ cup
bread flour	2 cups	3 cups	3½ cups
rapid or quick yeast	1½ tsp.	2 tsp.	2 tsp.
flour equivalent	*2 cups*	*3 cups*	*3½ cups*
cycle	*white, sweet; no timer*		
setting	*light to medium*		

per 1 oz. *57 calories, 1.9 g protein, 10.9 g carbohydrate, 0.6 g fat, 0 mg cholesterol, 107 mg sodium*

CARLIN'S DILLY BREAD

CARLIN NERHUS

Carlin says this bread has been a favorite of hers since childhood. She now has her husband and extended family hooked on it as well. Adjust with water or flour as needed only after a full 10 minutes of kneading. This is a high rising loaf of bread. I cut Carlin's yeast and egg amounts in half. If you have a 1¼ lb. machine (Seiko), make only the 1 lb. size to prevent overflows.

	1 lb.	**1½ lb.**	**2 lb.**
water	2 tbs.	3 tbs.	¼ cup
cottage cheese	¾ cup	1 cup	1¼ cups
eggs	1	2	2
salt	½ tsp.	1-1½ tsp.	1-1½ tsp.
dill seed	1½ tbs.	2 tbs.	2½ tbs.
instant onion	1½ tbs.	2 tbs.	2½ tbs.
sugar	2 tbs.	2½ tbs.	3 tbs.
baking soda	½ tsp.	½ tsp.	1 tsp.
bread flour	2 cups	3 cups	3½ cups
rapid or quick yeast	1 tsp.	1½ tsp.	1½ tsp.
flour equivalent	*2 cups*	*3 cups*	*3½ cups*
cycle	*white, sweet; no timer*		
setting	*light*		

per 1 oz. 73 calories, 3.5 g protein, 12.4 g carbohydrate, 0.7 g fat, 15 mg cholesterol, 137 mg sodium

MULTI-GRAIN BREADS

SO MANY GRAINS BREAD

RONA WALTZER

Rona developed this recipe, and you will enjoy its texture and unique, flavorful taste.

	1 lb.	**1½ lb.**	**2 lb.**
water	¾ cup.	1⅛ cups	1½ cups
vegetable oil	1 tbs.	1½ tbs.	2 tbs.
molasses or honey	2 tbs.	3 tbs.	4 tbs.
salt	½ tsp.	¾ tsp.	1 tsp.
bread flour	¾ cup	1⅛ cups	1½ cups
whole wheat flour	¾ cup	1⅛ cups	1½ cups
buckwheat flour	2 tbs.	3 tbs.	¼ cup
rye flour	2 tbs.	3 tbs.	¼ cup
soy flour	2 tbs.	3 tbs.	¼ cup
yellow cornmeal	2 tbs.	3 tbs.	¼ cup
rolled oats	¼ cup	⅓ cup	½ cup
vital gluten, optional	1 tbs.	1½ tbs.	2 tbs.
rapid or quick yeast	1 tsp.	1½ tsp.	2 tsp.
flour equivalent	*2¼ cups*	*3⅓ cups*	*4½ cups*
cycle	*wheat, white, sweet; timer*		
setting	*light to medium*		

per 1 oz.   *65 calories, 2.4 g protein, 11.7 g carbohydrate, 1.3 g fat, 0 mg cholesterol, 68 mg sodium*

KASHI RYE BREAD

HOWARD MULLER

Howard has adapted this recipe and is having trouble supplying all the requests for samples. Kashi (uncooked breakfast pilaf) is usually found with cereals in grocery stores. This recipe calls for cooked kashi.

	1 lb.	1½ lb.	1¾ lb.
water	½ cup	¾ cup	1 cup
margarine or vegetable oil	1 tbs.	1 tbs.	2 tbs.
sugar	1 tbs.	1½ tbs.	2 tbs.
salt	⅔ tsp.	1 tsp.	1 tsp.
caraway seeds	1 tsp.	1½ tsp.	2 tsp.
cooked kashi	⅓ cup	½ cup	⅔ cup
light rye flour	⅓ cup	½ cup	⅔ cup
bread flour	1⅓ cups	2 cups	2⅔ cups
rapid or quick yeast	1 tsp.	1½ tsp.	2 tsp.
flour equivalent	*2 cups*	*3 cups*	*4 cups*
cycle	*wheat, white, sweet; timer*		
setting	*medium*		

---

per 1 oz. *54 calories, 1.5 g protein, 9.6 g carbohydrate, 1 g fat, 0 mg cholesterol, 89 mg sodium*

ORANGE BRAN BREAD

I decreased the amount of bran in Mrs. Morrison's recipe, as it cuts the gluten's elastic network, which reduces the bread's rising. This has a nice flavor and rises nicely.

	1 lb.	1½ lb.	1¾ lb.
orange juice	⅞ cup (7 oz.)	1¼ cups	1¾ cups
butter or margarine	1 tbs.	1½ tbs.	2 tbs.
sugar	2 tbs.	3 tbs.	¼ cup
salt	¾ tsp.	1 tsp.	1 tsp.
orange peel	½ tsp.	¾ tsp.	1 tsp.
bread flour	1¾ cups	2¾ cups	3½ cups
wheat bran	¼ cup	⅓ cup	½ cup
dry milk, optional	1 tbs.	1½ tbs.	2 tbs.
vital gluten	1 tbs.	1½ tbs.	2 tbs.
rapid or quick yeast	1½ tsp.	2 tsp.	2 tsp.
*raisins	⅓ cup	½ cup	⅔ cup
flour equivalent	*2 cups*	*3 cups*	*4 cups*
cycle	*white, sweet; raisin*		
setting	*light to medium*		

*Add raisins at the beep or appropriate time for your machine.

per 1 oz. *173 calories, 16.9 g protein, 23.7 g carbohydrate, 2 g fat, 0 mg cholesterol, 111 mg sodium*

SHINGLETOWN RYE

Betty came up with this bread quite by accident. It was not quite what she was looking for (gingerbread) but one of the best tasting and best looking loaves of bread she has made. Use a yolk or white for the half egg. The ginger and cinnamon may be adjusted to taste.

	1 lb.	1½ lb.	2 lb.
water	⅔ cup	1 cup	1⅓ cups
egg	1	1½	2
vegetable oil	1 tbs.	2 tbs.	2½ tbs.
molasses	2 tbs.	3 tbs.	¼ cup
unsweetened cocoa	1 tbs.	1½ tbs.	2 tbs.
brown sugar	2 tsp.	1 tbs.	1½ tbs.
instant coffee granules	1 tsp.	1 tsp.	1½ tsp.
salt	¾ tsp.	1 tsp.	1 tsp.
ground ginger	¾ tsp.	1 tsp.	1¼ tsp.
cinnamon	¾ tsp.	1 tsp.	1¼ tsp.
rye flour	½ cup	¾ cup	1 cup
whole wheat flour	½ cup	¾ cup	1 cup

bread flour	1 cup	1½ cups	2 cups
vital gluten, optional	1 tbs.	1½ tbs.	2 tbs.
rapid or quick yeast	1 tsp.	1½ tsp.	2 tsp.
flour equivalent	*2 cups*	*3 cups*	*4 cups*
cycle	*wheat, white, sweet; no timer*		
setting	*light to medium*		

per 1 oz.   *70 calories, 2.4 g protein, 12.9 g carbohydrate, 1.2 g fat, 0 mg cholesterol, 107 mg sodium*

OLD WORLD RYE

RAE RUBIN

Rae has adapted this old-world rye recipe for her bread machine. She makes it on her quick cycle. Add the lemon juice 10 minutes after starting the machine — in all machines. If fresh buttermilk is on hand, substitute it for the water (cup for cup) and omit the dried buttermilk powder.

	1 lb.	1½ lb.	1¾ lb.
water	⅞ cup (7 oz.)	1 cup	1¼ cups
vegetable oil	2 tsp.	1 tbs.	1 tbs.
honey	2 tsp.	1 tbs.	1 tbs.
salt	½ tsp.	¾ tsp.	1 tsp.
baking soda	¼ tsp.	⅓ tsp.	½ tsp.
dried onion flakes	2 tsp.	2½ tsp.	1 tbs.
caraway seeds	2 tsp.	1 tbs.	1 tbs.
wheat germ	1 tbs.	1½ tbs.	2 tbs.
soy flour	1 tbs.	1½ tbs.	2 tbs.
whole wheat flour	⅔ cup	¾ cup	1 cup
rye flour	¼ cup	⅓ cup	½ cup
bread flour	1 cup	1½ cups	2 cups

buttermilk powder	2½ tbs.	3 tbs.	¼ cup
vital gluten, optional	1 tbs.	1½ tbs.	2 tbs.
rapid or quick yeast	1½ tsp.	1½ tsp.	2 tsp.
*lemon juice	2 tsp.	2½ tsp.	1 tbs.
flour equivalent	*2 cups*	*3 cups*	*4 cups*
cycle	*wheat, white, sweet; timer*		
setting	*light to medium*		

*Add 10 minutes after starting machine.

per 1 oz. *67 calories, 2.8 g protein, 12.1 g carbohydrate, 1 g fat, 1 mg cholesterol, 87 mg sodium*

RYE BREAD

PETER DAHL

The allspice really adds a unique, flavorful twist to this recipe developed by Peter Dahl. He listed it as an optional ingredient. Peter seems to be having quite a lot of fun developing recipes for his bread machine. All of his recipes are very low rising, dense breads with tremendous flavor. If you judge successful bread based on how high it rises in your pan, don't even try this. If you judge successful bread based on flavor and texture, you <u>must</u> try this. There is a lot of flour in this recipe, so watch the kneading and scrape the sides of the pan if necessary.

	1 lb.	1½ lb.	2 lb.
water	1⅛ cups	1½ cups	1¾ cups
vegetable oil	1 tbs.	1⅓ tbs.	2 tbs.
honey	1½ tbs.	2 tbs.	2½ tbs.
salt	¾ tsp.	1 tsp.	1 tsp.
ground allspice	¾ tsp.	1 tsp.	1 tsp.
caraway seed	2 tsp.	1 tbs.	1½ tbs.
bread flour	1½ cups	2 cups	2½ cups
rye flour	1½ cups	2 cups	2½ cups
vital gluten	2 tsp.	1 tbs.	1½ tbs.

| dry milk powder | 1½ tbs. | 2 tbs. | 2 tbs. |
| rapid or quick yeast | 2 tsp. | 2½ tsp. | 2½ tsp. |

flour equivalent	*3 cups*	*4 cups*	*5 cups*
cycle	*wheat, sweet, white; timer*		
setting	*medium*		

per 1 oz. 91 calories, 2.9 g protein, 17.4 g carbohydrate, 1.3 g fat, 0 mg cholesterol, 103 mg sodium

GRAPE NUTS BREAD

Jodi enjoys playing with recipes in her bread machine and developed this one. If your machine has difficulty baking properly with the large amount of raisins, cut them in half. I have received calls or letters from two people who have said that using Grape Nuts has scratched their machine pans. Neither I nor any testers have had this problem with Grape Nuts, but I mention it anyway. Remember that these pans are designed for nuts and other hard foods. Add the Grape Nuts in the order given or for DAK/Welbilt owners, put the flour in and then the Grape Nuts. Adjust water or flour if necessary.

	1 lb.	1½ lb.	2 lb.
water	⅔ cup	1 cup	1⅓ cups
butter or margarine	1 tbs.	1½ tbs.	2 tbs.
sugar	1½ tbs.	2 tbs.	3 tbs.
salt	½ tsp.	¾ tsp.	1 tsp.
cinnamon	¾ tsp.	1 tsp.	1½ tsp.
bread flour	1¾ cups	2¾ cups	3½ cups
Grape Nuts cereal	½ cup	¾ cup	1 cup
nonfat dry milk	1 tbs.	1½ tbs.	2 tbs.

rapid or quick yeast	1 tsp.	1½ tsp.	2 tsp.
*raisins	½ cup	¾ cup	1 cup
flour equivalent	*2¼ cups*	*3½ cups*	*4½ cups*
cycle	*white, sweet; timer*		
setting	*light to medium*		

*Add raisins at the beep or appropriate time for your machine.

per 1 oz.   83 calories, 2.3 g protein, 16.8 g carbohydrate, 1 g fat, 0 mg cholesterol, 103 mg sodium

HERE'S TO YOUR HEALTH

MARTHA BABCOCK

This is a recipe adaptation made for Martha. It results in a low-rising, moist, open grain loaf with lots of flavor. Watch the dough for moisture.

	1 lb.	1½ lb.	2 lb.
water	½ cup	¾ cup	1 cup
cottage cheese	⅓ cup	½ cup	⅔ cup
vegetable oil	1 tbs.	1½ tbs.	2 tbs.
honey	2 tbs.	3 tbs.	¼ cup
salt	⅓ tsp.	½ tsp.	⅔ tsp.
wheat germ	2 tbs.	3 tbs.	¼ cup
oats	¼ cup	⅓ cup	½ cup
whole wheat flour	¾ cup	1⅛ cups	1½ cups
bread flour	1⅛ cups	1⅔ cups	2¼ cups
rapid or quick yeast	1 tsp.	1½ tsp.	2 tsp.
*raisins	¼ cup	⅓ cup	½ cup
flour equivalent	*2¼ cups*	*3⅓ cups*	*4½ cups*
cycle	*white, sweet; timer*		
setting	*light to medium*		

*Add raisins at the beep or appropriate time for your machine.

per 1 oz. 81 calories, 2.9 g protein, 15.1 g carbohydrate, 1.3 g fat, 0 mg cholesterol, 65 mg sodium

SWEDISH RYE

JACK HILLER

Jack says that he prefers using powdered fennel seeds for this recipe which he adapted from a recipe of his mother, Myrtle. The fennel may be adjusted to taste. He heaps the sugar and adds water but I tested using the given amounts.

	1 lb.	**1½ lb.**	**1¾ lb.**
water	⅔ cup	1 cup	1⅓ cups
butter or margarine	3 tbs.	4 tbs.	5 tbs.
salt	½ tsp.	½ tsp.	1 tsp.
fennel seed	1½ tbs.	2 tbs.	2½ tbs.
sugar	3 tbs.	¼ cup	⅓ cup
rye flour	1 cup	1½ cups	2 cups
bread flour	1 cup	1½ cups	2 cups
vital gluten	1½ tbs.	2 tbs.	2½ tbs.
rapid or quick yeast	1½ tsp.	2 tsp.	2 tsp.
*candied or dried mixed fruit	¼ cup	⅓ cup	½ cup
flour equivalent	*2 cups*	*3 cups*	*4 cups*
cycle	*wheat, white, sweet; no timer*		
setting	*light to medium*		

*Add fruit at the beep or appropriate time for your machine

per 1 oz. *90 calories, 2.2 g protein, 15.3 g carbohydrate, 2.5 g fat, 0 mg cholesterol, 97 mg sodium*

MULTI-GRAIN BREAD

PUNKI GEHRING

Punki uses a 10 grain cereal for this flavorful loaf. As not all stores carry it, use either a 7, 9, 10 or 12 grain cereal as available. Apple juice concentrate may be used instead of the applesauce. Punki adds a tablespoon or two of water to adjust the texture of the dough. She uses the higher amount of salt, but I prefer less.

	1 lb.	**1½ lb.**	**1¾ lb.**
buttermilk	⅞ cup (7 oz.)	1¼ cups	1½ cups
applesauce	1½ tbs.	2 tbs.	3 tbs.
sugar	1½ tbs.	2 tbs.	2½ tbs.
salt	½-¾ tsp.	¾-1 tsp.	1 tsp.
10 grain cereal	½ cup	⅔ cup	¾ cup
bread flour	1½ cups	2 cups	2½ cups
whole wheat flour	¾ cup	1 cup	1⅛ cups
vital gluten	2 tbs.	3 tbs.	¼ cup
rapid or quick yeast	1½ tsp.	2 tsp.	2 tsp.
water	as needed	as needed	as needed
flour equivalent	*2¾ cups*	*3⅔ cups*	*4⅛ cups*
cycle	*wheat, white, sweet; no timer*		
setting	*medium*		

per 1 oz. *96 calories, 4 g protein, 18.2 g carbohydrate, 0.7 g fat, 0 mg cholesterol, 80 mg sodium*

WHOLE WHEAT IRISH SODA BREAD   FRANK RAWLINSON

Frank puts the raisins in the water, microwaves them for 2 minutes and then lets the raisins stand for at least 2 hours before straining them. The swollen, soft raisins spread into small particles throughout the loaf. Add the raisins with the liquids. I am lazy and add unplumped raisins at the beginning.

	1 lb.	**1½ lb.**	**1¾ lb.**
buttermilk	⅞ cup (7 oz.)	1⅛ cups	1½ cups
margarine or oil	1 tbs.	1½ tbs.	2 tbs.
honey	1 tbs.	1½ tbs.	2 tbs.
raisins	½ cup	¾ cup	1 cup
sugar	1 tbs.	1½ tbs.	2 tbs.
salt	½ tsp.	½ tsp.	1 tsp.
baking soda	½ tsp.	½ tsp.	1 tsp.
bread flour	1½ cups	2¼ cups	3 cups
whole wheat flour	½ cup	¾ cup	1 cup
vital gluten, optional	1 tbs.	1½ tbs.	2 tbs.
rapid dry yeast	1½ tsp.	2 tsp.	2 tsp.
flour equivalent	*2 cups*	*3 cups*	*4 cups*
cycle	*wheat, white, sweet; timer*		
setting	*medium*		

per 1 oz. 87 calories, 2.9 g protein, 16.7 g carbohydrate, 1.2 g fat, 0 mg cholesterol, 106 mg sodium

SUNFLOWER BRAN BREAD

R.M. OLMSTEAD

R.M. Olmstead developed this tasty treat. I use oil instead of butter so the molasses slides off the same measuring spoon. The recipe states fine bran flakes — I use bran, not bran cereal. I cut the salt amount in half.

	1 lb.	1½ lb.	1¾ lb.
water	¾ cup	1¼ cups	1½ cups
butter or oil	1 tbs.	1½ tbs.	1½ tbs.
molasses	1½ tbs.	2 tbs.	2½ tbs.
salt	½ tsp.	¾ tsp.	1 tsp.
bran (wheat or oat)	½ cup	¾ cup	1 cup
sunflower kernels	¼ cup	⅓ cup	⅓ cup
bread flour	2 cups	3 cups	3½ cups
rapid or quick yeast	2 tsp.	2 tsp.	2½ tsp.
flour equivalent	*2½ cups*	*3¾ cups*	*4½ cups*
cycle	*wheat, white, sweet; timer*		
setting	*medium*		

per 1 oz.   *77 calories, 2.6 g protein, 12.4 g carbohydrate, 2.3 g fat, 0 mg cholesterol, 68 mg sodium*

SEEDED WHEAT BREAD

MARGARET CURTIS

Margaret used to make this by hand. She uses honey crunch wheat germ. Amaranth and teff give it lots of nutrition and a special nutty flavor. I reduced the amount of salt.

	1 lb.	**1½ lb.**	**1¾ lb.**
milk	3 tbs.	¼ cup	⅓ cup
water	⅝ cup (5 oz.)	⅞ cup (7 oz.)	1¼ cups
butter or margarine	1 tbs.	1½ tbs.	2 tbs.
sugar	2 tbs.	3 tbs.	¼ cup
salt	½ tsp.	¾ tsp.	1-1½ tsp.
wheat germ	1½ tbs.	2 tbs.	2½ tbs.
teff grains or seeds	1½ tbs.	2 tbs.	2½ tbs.
amaranth grains	2 tsp.	1 tbs.	1⅓ tbs.
vital wheat gluten	2 tsp.	1 tbs.	1⅓ tbs.
whole wheat flour	⅓ cup	½ cup	⅔ cup
bread flour	1⅔ cups	2½ cups	3⅓ cups
rapid rise yeast	1 tsp.	1½ tsp.	2 tsp.
flour equivalent	*2+ cups*	*3+ cups*	*4+ cups*
cycle	*wheat, white, sweet; timer*		
setting	*light to medium*		

per 1 oz.   98 calories, 3.7 g protein, 17.8 g carbohydrate, 1.7 g fat, 0 mg cholesterol, 172 mg sodium

WHOLE WHEAT SANDWICH BREAD   ERMA AUTENRIETH

Erma says that she has had difficulty perfecting a whole wheat bread which would hold up to her meat and lettuce sandwiches. She finally perfected it and is ready to share it with us. This is a dense, low-rising loaf which slices well.

	1 lb.	**1½ lb.**	**1¾ lb.**
water	¾ cup	1⅛ cups	1½ cups
corn oil	2 tbs.	3 tbs.	¼ cup
sugar	2 tsp.	1 tbs.	1⅓ tbs.
salt	½ tsp.	1 tsp.	1 tsp.
whole wheat flour	1 cup	1¼ cups	1¾ cups
bread flour	1¼ cups	1¾ cups	2⅓ cups
dry milk powder	1½ tbs.	2 tbs.	2½ tbs.
rapid or quick yeast	1½ tsp.	2 tsp.	2 tsp.
flour equivalent	*2¼ cups*	*3 cups*	*4⅛ cups*
cycle	*wheat, white, sweet; timer*		
setting	*medium*		

per 1 oz. 75 calories, 2.3 g protein, 12.5 g carbohydrate, 2 g fat, 0 mg cholesterol, 70 mg sodium

GERMAN RYE BREAD

SHERRY LIBSACK

Sherry has adapted her mother-in-law's light and airy rye recipe for her bread machine. One of the secrets is the vital gluten which may be found in some large grocery stores or in most health food stores.

	1 lb.	1½ lb.	2 lb.
water	⅞ cup	1⅓ cups	1⅔ cups
sugar	1½ tbs.	2 tbs.	2½ tbs.
salt	⅓ tsp.	½ tsp.	⅔ tsp.
bread flour	2 cups	3 cups	3½ cups
rye flour	⅓ cup	½ cup	½ cup
vital gluten	2 tsp.	1 tbs.	1 tbs.
rapid or quick yeast	1½ tsp.	2 tsp.	2 tsp.
flour equivalent	*2⅓ cups*	*3½ cups*	*4 cups*
cycle	*white, wheat, sweet; timer*		
setting	*medium*		

---

per 1 oz.   65 calories, 2.4 g protein, 13.1 g carbohydrate, 0.3 g fat, 0 mg cholesterol, 45 mg sodium

CHOCOLATE CREAM OF WHEAT BREAD MARTHA PUNCHES

Martha has several blue ribbons from the Pennsylvania State Fair for breads made in her pre-machine days. If your machine is prone to the doughy blues, cut the amount of sugar to 3 tbs., ¼ cup or ⅓ cup. The dough starts out looking very wet but it does form a ball after about 10 minutes of kneading.

	1 lb.	**1½ lb.**	**2 lb.**
milk	⅔ cup	1 cup	1⅓ cups
butter or margarine	2 tbs.	3 tbs.	4 tbs.
eggs	1	1½	2
salt	1 tsp.	1-1½ tsp.	1-2 tsp.
sugar	¼ cup	⅓ cup	½ cup
unsweetened cocoa	1 tbs.	1½ tbs.	2 tbs.
cream of wheat, uncooked	⅔ cup	1 cup	1⅓ cups
bread flour	1⅓ cups	2 cups	2⅔ cups
rapid or quick yeast	1 tsp.	1½ tsp.	2 tsp.
*chocolate chips, optional	¼ cup	⅓ cup	½ cup
flour equivalent	*2 cups*	*3 cups*	*4 cups*
cycle	*white, sweet, raisin; no timer*		
setting	*light*		

*Add chocolate chips at the beep or appropriate time for your machine.

per 1 oz. *71 calories, 2 g protein, 11.7 g carbohydrate, 1.9 g fat, 1 mg cholesterol, 175 mg sodium*

JERRY'S DAILY BREAD

JERRY SNELLING

Jerry says this is truly his daily bread — reliable, basic and so very good! The sunflower kernels could also be added at the appropriate time for raisins. He uses gluten flour but I used vital gluten for testing. The loaf rises moderately well.

	1 lb.	**1½ lb.**	**1¾ lb.**
water	⅔ cup	1⅛ cups	1¼ cups
vegetable oil	1 tbs.	1½ tbs.	2 tbs.
honey	1 tbs.	1½ tbs.	2 tbs.
molasses	1 tbs.	1½ tbs.	2 tbs.
salt	½ tsp.	¾ tsp.	1 tsp.
bread flour	1⅓ cups	2 cups	2¼ cups
whole wheat flour	⅔ cup	1 cup	1¼ cups
vital gluten	1 tbs.	1½ tbs.	2 tbs.
dry milk powder	1½ tbs.	2 tbs.	3 tbs.
sunflower kernels	3 tbs.	¼ cup	⅓ cup
rapid or quick yeast	1 tsp.	1½ tsp.	2 tsp.
flour equivalent	*2 cups*	*3 cups*	*3½ cups*
cycle	*white, sweet, wheat; timer*		
setting	*light to medium*		

per 1 oz. *79 calories, 2.8 g protein, 13 g carbohydrate, 2 g fat, 0 mg cholesterol, 70 mg sodium*

MULTI-GRAIN RAISIN BREAD

CAROL ANN JOHNSON

I cut Carol Ann's amount of oil in half to avoid the doughy blues. The cinnamon may be adjusted to taste. This has a moderate rise and may be somewhat dense.

	1 lb.	1½ lb.	1¾ lb.
water	1 cup	1⅓ cups	1½ cups
vegetable oil	1½ tbs.	2 tbs.	3 tbs.
honey	3 tbs.	¼ cup	⅓ cup
salt	¾ tsp.	1 tsp.	1 tsp.
cinnamon	1½ tsp.	2 tsp.	1 tbs.
bread flour	1½ cups	2 cups	2½ cups
whole wheat flour	¾ cup	1 cup	1¼ cups
oat bran	¼ cup	⅓ cup	½ cup
vital gluten, optional	1½ tbs.	2 tbs.	2½ tbs.
rapid or quick yeast	1½ tsp.	2 tsp.	2 tsp.
*raisins	½ cup	⅔ cup	¾ cup
flour equivalent	*2½ cups*	*3⅓ cups*	*4¼ cups*
cycle	*wheat, sweet, white; no timer*		
setting	*light*		

*Add raisins at the beep or appropriate time for your machine.

per 1 oz. *101 calories, 3 g protein, 20 g carbohydrate, 1.7 g fat, 0 mg cholesterol, 102 mg sodium*

PORCUPINE BREAD

FLARANE WOLD

Flarane says that her husband makes this but says that sometimes it's difficult to find a porcupine!

	1 lb.	**1½ lb.**	**2 lb.**
water	⅞ cup (7 oz.)	1⅛ cups	1⅓ cups
vegetable oil	2 tsp.	1 tbs.	1 tbs.
salt	½ tsp.	¾ tsp.	1 tsp.
sugar	1 tbs.	1½ tbs.	2 tbs.
sesame seeds	1½ tbs.	2 tbs.	3 tbs.
sunflower seeds	2 tbs.	3 tbs.	¼ cup
rolled oats	⅓ cup	½ cup	½ cup
bread flour	2 cups	3 cups	3½ cups
rapid or quick yeast	1½ tsp.	2 tsp.	2 tsp.
*raisins, optional	¼ cup	⅓ cup	½ cup
flour equivalent	2⅓ cups	3½ cups	4 cups
cycle	*white, sweet; timer*		
setting	*medium*		

*Add raisins at the beep or appropriate time for your machine.

per 1 oz. *125 calories, 4.3 g protein, 19.6 g carbohydrate, 3.3 g fat, 0 mg cholesterol, 144 mg sodium*

CATSKILL RYE

DONNA CELEIRO

Donna developed this high rising, light and fluffy rye bread. I cut her salt and yeast in half and slightly decreased the nonfat dry milk. One trick to achieve a high rising rye is increasing the amount of flour. If necessary, scrape the sides of the pan with a rubber spatula, pushing the ingredients into the middle.

	1 lb.	**1½ lb.**	**2 lb.**
water	1 cup	1¼ cups	1⅔ cups
vegetable oil	1 tbs.	1⅓ tbs.	1½ tbs.
honey	2 tbs.	2½ tbs.	3 tbs.
salt	½ tsp.	⅔ tsp.	1 tsp.
caraway seeds	1 tbs.	1⅓ tbs.	1½ tbs.
rye flour	1 cup	1¼ cups	1½ cups
bread flour	1¾ cups	2¼ cups	3⅔ cups
nonfat dry milk	2 tbs.	2½ tbs.	3 tbs.
vital gluten	¼ cup	5 tbs.	⅓ cup
rapid or quick yeast	1½ tsp.	2 tsp.	2½ tsp.
flour equivalent	*3 cups*	*3⅔ cups*	*5⅔ cups*
cycle	*wheat, white, sweet; no timer*		
setting	*light*		

per 1 oz.   88 calories, 2.9 g protein, 16.8 g carbohydrate, 1.3 g fat, 0 mg cholesterol, 71 mg sodium

GOLDEN HONEY CORN BREAD

BETH DASH KORUITZ

Beth developed a winner with this delicious corn bread. The potato flakes and the cornmeal make a great combination.

	1 lb.	1½ lb.	2 lb.
water	⅞ cup (7 oz.)	1¼ cups	1½ cups
canola oil	1 tbs.	1⅓ tbs.	1½ tbs.
honey	1 tbs.	1½ tbs.	2 tbs.
salt	¾ tsp.	1 tsp.	1 tsp.
cornmeal	¼ cup	⅓ cup	½ cup
instant potato flakes	¼ cup	⅓ cup	½ cup
bread flour	2 cups	3 cups	3½ cups
milk powder	1 tbs.	1½ tbs.	2 tbs.
rapid or quick yeast	1 tsp.	1½ tsp.	2 tsp.
flour equivalent	*2½ cups*	*3⅔ cups*	*4½ cups*
cycle	*white; timer*		
setting	*medium*		

---

per 1 oz. 72 calories, 2.1 g protein, 13.4 g carbohydrate, 1.2 g fat, 0 mg cholesterol, 103 mg sodium

OATMEAL BREAD

Martha makes the large recipe in her machine on the dough cycle and then bakes two loaves in her oven! Use an egg white or yolk for the half egg. I cut the amount of milk, salt and yeast.

	1 lb.	**1½ lb.**	**2 lb.**
milk	⅔ cup	¾ cup	1 cup
applesauce	2½ tbs.	¼ cup	⅓ cup
egg	½	1	1½
sugar	1½ tbs.	2 tbs.	2½ tbs.
salt	½ tsp.	1 tsp.	1 tsp.
oats	1 cup	1½ cups	2 cups
bread flour	1¾ cups	2 cups	2⅔ cups
vital gluten	1 tbs.	1½ tbs.	2 tbs.
rapid or quick yeast	1 tsp.	1½ tsp.	2 tsp.
flour equivalent	*2¾ cups*	*3½ cups*	*4⅔ cups*
cycle	*sweet, white; no timer*		
setting	*medium*		

per 1 oz.   77 calories, 3.2 g protein, 14.5 g carbohydrate, 0.8 g fat, 1 mg cholesterol, 74 mg sodium

COTTAGE CHEESE WHEAT BREAD MARGARET NELSON

Margaret uses small curd cottage cheese in this bread which has much body and moisture. Cottage cheese can be finicky as a main liquid contributor to dough — watch the dough and adjust with water or flour as necessary. If you have a 1¼ lb. machine manufactured by Seiko, use the 1 lb. recipe to prevent overflows.

	1 lb.	**1½ lb.**	**2 lb. *only***
cottage cheese	1 cup	1½ cups	1⅔ cups
egg	1	1	2
butter or margarine	1 tbs.	1½ tbs.	1½ tbs.
dill weed	1 tsp.	1½ tsp.	1½ tsp.
baking soda	¼ tsp.	½ tsp.	½ tsp.
salt	½ tsp.	1 tsp.	1 tsp.
sugar	1 tbs.	1 tbs.	2 tbs.
bread flour	2 cups	3 cups	3½ cups
whole wheat flour	¼ cup	⅓ cup	½ cup
rapid or quick yeast	1 tsp.	1½ tsp.	2 tsp.
flour equivalent	*2¼ cups*	*3⅓ cups*	*4 cups*
cycle	*whole wheat, sweet, white; no timer*		
setting	*medium*		

per 1 oz.   85 calories, 4.1 g protein, 12.8 g carbohydrate, 1.9 g fat, 15 mg cholesterol, 205 mg sodium

MOLASSES WHEAT BREAD

Quentin says he sometimes adds raisins and/or walnuts for variety.

	1 lb.	1½ lb.	2 lb.
water	¾ cup	1 cup	1½ cups
vegetable oil	½ tbs.	1 tbs.	1½ tbs.
molasses, or maple or corn syrup	1½ tbs.	2 tbs.	2½ tbs.
honey	1½ tbs.	2 tbs.	2½ tbs.
egg	½	1	1
salt	¾ tsp.	1 tsp.	1 tsp.
wheat germ	3 tbs.	¼ cup	⅓ cup
whole bran cereal	3 tbs.	¼ cup	⅓ cup
rolled oats	3 tbs.	¼ cup	⅓ cup
whole wheat flour	1⅛ cups	1½ cups	2 cups
bread flour	1⅛ cups	1½ cups	2 cups
dry milk powder	3 tbs.	¼ cup	⅓ cup
vital gluten, optional	1½ tbs.	2 tbs.	2 tbs.
rapid or quick yeast	1½ tsp.	2 tsp.	2 tsp.
flour equivalent	*2½ cups*	*3¾ cups*	*5 cups*
cycle	*wheat, white, sweet; timer*		
setting	*light*		

per 1 oz.   *98 calories, 4.2 g protein, 19.7 g carbohydrate, 1.2 g fat, 0 mg cholesterol, 141 mg sodium*

CRACKED WHEAT BREAD

CAMILLE CARTER

Camille says that this is her very favorite all purpose bread and she bakes it at least once a week. She has also used the recipe for dinner rolls and has received rave reviews. Soak the cracked wheat for at least 1 hour before adding to pan with remaining ingredients. Adjust dough as necessary with milk or flour.

	1 lb.	**1½ lb.**	**1¾ lb.**
boiling water	½ cup	⅔ cup	1 cup
cracked wheat	½ cup	⅔ cup	1 cup
soak at least 1 hour			
milk	½ cup	½ cup	⅔ cup
vegetable or canola oil	1 tbs.	1½ tbs.	2 tbs.
honey	1 tbs.	1½ tbs.	2 tbs.
salt	½ tsp.	¾ tsp.	1 tsp.
bread flour	2 cups	2½ cups	3 cups
rapid or quick yeast	1½ tsp.	2 tsp.	2½ tsp.
flour equivalent	*2½ cups*	*3⅓ cups*	*4 cups*
cycle	*wheat, sweet, white; no timer - adjust consistency*		
setting	*medium*		

per 1 oz. *69 calories, 2.2 g protein, 12.3 g carbohydrate, 1.3 g fat, 1 mg cholesterol, 71 mg sodium*

OAT SUNFLOWER MILLET BREAD

CARL KIELMANN

Carl, a retired banker, first had similar rolls from a bakery in Jackson Hole, Wyoming. He has figured out the recipe for his bread machine. This moist, flavorful bread was a real hit with many tasters. I cut back on the amount of salt to soften the crust a little bit. Carl generally adds walnuts but any nut could be used. This moist dough may be prone to the doughy blues in the glass domed machines — make the 1½ lb. size and not the 2 lb.

	1 lb.	**1½ lb.**	**2 lb. *only***
water	¾ cup	1⅛ cups	1½ cups
canola oil	¼ cup	⅓ cup	½ cup
honey	3 tbs.	¼ cup	⅓ cup
sugar	3 tbs.	¼ cup	⅓ cup
salt	½ tsp.	¾ tsp.	1 tsp.
millet	2 tbs.	3 tbs.	¼ cup
sunflower kernels	1 tbs.	1½ tbs.	2 tbs.
chopped nuts	2 tbs.	3 tbs.	¼ cup
rolled oats	2½ tbs.	¼ cup	⅓ cup
whole wheat flour	½ cup	¾ cup	1 cup

bread flour	1½ cups	2⅓ cups	3 cups
dry milk powder	1 tbs.	1½ tbs.	2 tbs.
rapid or quick yeast	1 tsp.	1½ tsp.	1½ tsp.

flour equivalent	*2¼ cups*	*3⅓ cups*	*4½ cups*
cycle	*wheat, sweet, white; timer*		
setting	*light*		

per 1 oz. *117 calories, 2.5 g protein, 17.3 g carbohydrate, 4.6 g fat, 0 mg cholesterol, 69 mg sodium*

DOUGH CYCLE

Recipes in this chapter are given in one size only. All machines, whether 1 lb. or 2 lb., will successfully knead (but not bake) this amount of dough. If you have a 1 lb. machine, you may want to watch the dough and puncture it with a bamboo skewer if it starts to rise over the top of the machine pan (I only had this happen one time out of all the testing done).

If you have a Welbilt ABM 100 or DAK machine, these recipes were tested using the basic (white) manual setting with one kneading and rising only. The first kneading is about 20 minutes and the rising is about 1 hour. The machine was then turned off and the dough removed. Testing indicated that allowing the machine to go through the full second kneading made the dough too airy and difficult to roll or shape. Testing was done on all other machines on the regular dough cycle.

Once the dough is removed from the machine, it is helpful to lightly flour both your hands and the counter (or board). I find it helpful to have a little flour in my hand when I reach into the machine pan and pull the dough from the bottom. The extra flour at this point makes the dough less sticky and allows me to remove all the dough easily. Use only enough flour to allow you to shape it. The softer the dough, the lighter and fluffier the texture of the finished product. It is not necessary to knead the dough after removing it from the machine. The dough is only punched down during the shaping process.

You probably know of several ways to shape rolls. Here are two simple ideas. First, you can break off a given number of pieces and roll them into balls. Or, you can roll the dough into a rectangle, roll it up starting at the wide end and then cut the dough into a given number of pieces. Rolls may be placed either on a lightly greased baking sheet or muffin tin and baked according to directions.

WALNUT STICKY BUNS

CARYN HART

Caryn shares a favorite recipe adapted to the machines. How deliciously deca-dent! Caryn uses kosher salt in this, but sea salt or regular salt may be used also. Makes 12.

DOUGH

¾ cup milk
2 tbs. butter or margarine
1 egg
½ tsp. salt

½ cup sugar
2½ cups bread flour
1½ tsp. rapid or quick yeast

Put dough ingredients in machine and start the dough cycle. Mix filling ingredients together and divide in half. Distribute half of the filling among 12 muffin pan cups which have been sprayed with nonstick vegetable spray and set aside. Remove dough from machine and roll into a large rectangle. Flour the work surface and/or the dough if necessary to prevent sticking. Spread remaining filling over dough and roll into a jelly roll starting with the wide end. Cut roll into 12 equal pieces and place in muffin cups on top of first half of filling. Let rise in a warm, draft-free location for 35 to 45 minutes. Bake in a preheated 375° oven for 20 minutes. Turn pan over to release buns while still hot.

FILLING

6 tbs. butter or margarine
2½ tbs. honey
1 cup brown sugar
½ tsp. cinnamon
1 tsp. all purpose or bread flour
2 cups chopped walnuts

Melt butter, add remaining ingredients and mix together.

per bun *402 calories, 9 g protein, 50.1 g carbohydrate, 20.1 g fat, 1 mg cholesterol, 209 mg sodium*

POPPY SEED ROLLS

Woody makes these delicious rolls and shares the recipe with us. Woody does not use the sugar, but I like it. The choice is yours!

1⅓ cups water
3 tbs. olive oil
1 tsp. salt
1 tbs. poppy seeds
1½ tsp. sugar, optional
3½ cups bread flour
¼ cup dry milk powder
2 tsp. rapid or quick yeast

At the end of the dough cycle, remove dough, form into rolls (see page 145) and place on a greased baking sheet. Cover and allow to rise in a warm, draft-free location for 1 hour. Bake in a preheated 375° oven for 12 to 15 minutes or until lightly browned.

---

per 1 oz.   157 calories, 4.9 g protein, 24.7 g carbohydrate, 4.3 g fat, 0 mg cholesterol, 187 mg sodium

BAKED PORTZELKA

BILL ASHMAN

Bill adapted this recipe from a deep fat fried recipe handed down from his grandmother. He remembers them as a special treat and hopes that his grandmother would approve of his changes to make them with less fat. Bill uses less flour but then adds more by hand after the machine has stopped. I added some at the beginning. I added some orange peel (½-1 tsp.) to one test group and used dried cranberries instead of the raisins — Mmmmm.

5 oz. evaporated milk
2 eggs
2 tbs. butter or margarine
¼ cup sugar
½ tsp. salt

2-2⅓ cups bread flour
1 tsp. rapid or quick yeast
½ cup raisins
glaze: 1 egg, beaten with 1 tbs. water

The raisins should be added to all machines 10 minutes after the dough cycle is started. Remove dough from the machine at the completion of the dough cycle. Break and shape dough into small, ping-pong-sized balls and place on a greased baking sheet. Cover and let rise for 1½ hours. Brush tops with glaze and bake in a preheated 350° oven for 12 to 15 minutes.

per 1 oz.   137 calories, 4 g protein, 23.7 g carbohydrate, 3.2 g fat, 3 mg cholesterol, 137 mg sodium

ZAHTAR PITA

Gloria uses zahtar, a Middle Eastern spice blend which consists of the dried, ground berries of the sumac bush, roasted sesame seeds and thyme. Pita bread is usually cut into small triangles and the cut end of the pita is dipped in olive oil and then in the zahtar blend. Zahtar is available from Middle Eastern stores, or simply substitute thyme or oregano. Nutritional information was unavailable for zahtar so ground thyme was used. The secret to good pitas is a really hot oven.

1⅛ cups water
1 tbs. olive oil
1 tbs. zahtar, or oregano or thyme
1 tbs. sugar

1 tsp. salt
3 cups bread flour
1½ tsp. rapid or quick yeast

Remove dough from the machine at the completion of the dough cycle and divide into about 8 pieces. Flatten each piece by hand into a small circle about 6 inches in diameter and place on a greased baking sheet. Cover and let rise for 30 minutes. Brush top with a little olive oil and bake in a preheated 500° oven for 8 to 10 minutes.

---

per pita   161 calories, 4.8 g protein, 28.8 g carbohydrate, 3.0 g fat, 0 mg cholesterol, 268 mg sodium

TACO PITA POCKETS

DENISE BRADSHAW

Denise says her husband <u>really</u> likes these pockets and it's a bit less messy than tacos with traditional shells. Stuff the pockets with your favorite taco fixings or serve as a side bread with chili. The key to the pitas puffing is a very hot oven, so preheat it for at least 30 minutes or more.

¾ cup water
¼ cup taco sauce, or salsa
2 tbs. vegetable oil
1 tbs. sugar
½ tsp. salt

1½ tbs. taco seasoning
1½ cups bread flour
1 cup whole wheat flour
1½ tsp. rapid or quick yeast

Remove dough from the machine at the completion of the dough cycle. Divide into 6 or 8 balls, and flatten each ball with a rolling pin to make a 6-inch circle. Place on a cornmeal-covered baking sheet, cover and let rise for 30 minutes. Slide pitas off baking sheet onto a pizza stone, bake directly on oven rack or bake on baking sheet. Bake at 500° for about 8 minutes or until golden brown. Remove and place in a closed paper bag until cool.

---

per 1 oz. 119 calories, 2.9 g protein, 17.8 g carbohydrate, 4.1 g fat, 0 mg cholesterol, 151 mg sodium

HOT CROSS BUNS

DEBBIE WOODARD

Hot cross buns are traditionally served during the week preceding Easter, especially on Good Friday. These are really good any time of the year. Golden raisins, currants, dried cranberries or dried blueberries may be substituted for the raisins.

1 cup milk
2 eggs
1 tsp. vanilla extract
2 tbs. butter or margarine
¾ cup raisins
½-1 tsp. cinnamon

½ cup sugar
1 tsp. salt
4 cups bread flour or all purpose flour
1½ tsp. rapid or quick yeast
glaze: 1 egg yolk, beaten with 1 tbs.
  water

Remove dough from the machine at the completion of the dough cycle. Break into pieces of dough about the size of an egg. Roll each piece into a ball and place on a greased baking sheet. Cover with a towel and place in a warm, draft-free location for about ½ hour. Brush tops with glaze. Bake in a preheated 375° oven for about 25 minutes or until golden brown. Allow to cool and then drizzle frosting over tops in the form of a cross.

FROSTING

¼-½ cup confectioners' sugar
¼-½ tsp. vanilla or lemon extract
1-2 tbs. milk

Mix ingredients together, using enough milk to achieve a good consistency.

per 1 oz. *242 calories, 6.5 g protein, 48 g carbohydrate, 3.1 g fat, 2 mg cholesterol, 225 mg sodium*

CRANBERRY BUNS

LARRY BENNETT

These buns are a great treat for breakfast or any time of the day, especially during the holiday season! There is no substitute for piping hot buns right out of the oven. Apple juice or cranapple juice may be used in place of the cranberry juice. Idea: Place the buns around the outer edge of a pizza pan and make an edible wreath for holiday entertaining.

1½ cups cranberry juice
2 tbs. butter or margarine
2 tbs. brown sugar
½-1 tsp. cinnamon
¼ tsp. nutmeg
½-1 tsp. salt
4 cups bread flour
2 tsp. rapid or quick yeast

Remove dough from the machine and roll into a large rectangle. Spread filling ingredients on top and roll in a jelly roll fashion starting at the wide end. Cut roll into 1-inch-wide segments and lay on a greased baking sheet. Brush top with melted butter if desired. Bake in a preheated 350° oven for 20 to 30 minutes or until golden brown.

FILLING

½ cup brown sugar
2 tbs. cinnamon
⅔ cup dried cranberries, or raisins
½ cup chopped nuts (walnuts or pecans)
4 tbs. melted butter

Mix ingredients together.

---

per 1 oz.   *229 calories, 4.9 g protein, 38.1 g carbohydrate, 7.1 g fat, 8 mg cholesterol, 185 mg sodium*

VEGETARIAN-STUFFED PIZZA

MRS. EDWIN T. WRIGHT

Mrs. Wright makes the dough for this great pizza in her bread machine. She makes a pizza sauce from tomato sauce simmered for just a few minutes with some basil. Prepared pizza sauces could also be used. If using frozen vegetables, thaw and drain. I confess that I used a full 16 oz. bag of frozen broccoli and cauliflower (3 cups) and 2 cups of cheese.

1½ cups warm water
2 tbs. vegetable or olive oil
1 tsp. salt
1 tsp. sugar

1 cup whole wheat flour
2⅓-2½ cups bread flour
1 pkg. (2¼ tsp.) rapid or quick yeast
glaze: beaten egg or pizza sauce

Preheat oven to 375°. Sprinkle a greased 12-inch pizza pan with 1 tbs. cornmeal. Remove dough from the machine. Roll ⅔ dough into 14-inch circle and place on a 12-inch pan. Mix together filling ingredients and spoon over dough, leaving a 2-inch border. Roll remaining dough into a 14-inch circle and place on top. Fold edges over and crimp, sealing shut. Slit top with fork or sharp knife in 4 or 5 places. Brush with beaten egg or pizza sauce and bake for 25 to 35 minutes or until top is golden. If you did not bake pizza sauce on pizza, warm it and pour over baked pizza when serving.

FILLING

2-3 cups shredded mozzarella
1 cup broccoli florets
1 cup cauliflower florets
½-1 tsp. oregano, to taste

per ⅛ pie   375 calories, 22.9 g protein, 40.2 g carbohydrate, 14.1 g fat, 31 mg cholesterol, 571 mg sodium

CINNAMON MONKEY BREAD

LORRAINE PETRASEK

Lorraine now uses her Panasonic machine to make this old family favorite. She either uses her dough cycle and makes the monkey bread or she removes the dough, rolls it as a jelly-roll, fills it with cottage and cream cheeses and returns it to her machine for further baking. This variety cycle is only on the National and Panasonic machines. The craisins are a variation which is fun for fall or winter entertaining.

DOUGH

1/4 cup water
1 cup milk
1/3 cup butter
1/3 cup sugar
1 tsp. salt
2 eggs
3 1/2-3 3/4 cups bread flour
2 tsp. rapid or quick yeast

Upon completion of dough cycle, divide dough into small balls (just smaller than an egg) and dip into melted butter and then into sugar mixture. Put in a greased tube or loaf pan, cover with a towel and let rise in a warm, draft-free location for 30 to 40 minutes. Bake in a preheated 375° oven for about 45 minutes.

COATING

½ cup butter
1 cup sugar
1½ tsp. cinnamon
1 cup finely chopped nuts
½ cup raisins *or craisins*

Melt butter. Mix remaining ingredients together in a small bowl.

---

per 1 oz. *309 calories, 6.3 g protein, 40 g carbohydrate, 14.7 g fat, 1 mg cholesterol, 276 mg sodium*

DINNER ROLLS

KAREN SWANSON

Karen won a blue ribbon at the state fair for this recipe! She makes her own multi-grain flour blend, but there are blends available in health food stores or mail order catalogs. Makes 12 rolls.

1 cup warm water
1 egg
3 tbs. vegetable oil
3 tbs. sugar
1 tsp. salt
2 cups bread flour
1 cup multi-grain flour
1/3 cup dry milk powder
2 tsp. rapid or quick yeast

Upon completion of the dough cycle, remove dough and form rolls, place on a greased baking sheet, cover with a towel and let rise in a warm, draft-free location for 30 to 40 minutes. Bake in a preheated 400° oven for 15 to 18 minutes.

per roll   164 calories, 5.7 g protein, 26.2 g carbohydrate, 4.5 g fat, 18 mg cholesterol, 194 mg sodium

HARD ROLLS

KAREN SWANSON

Karen won <u>another</u> blue ribbon at the state fair for these hard rolls. Makes 12 delicious rolls.

1¼ cups warm water
1 egg white
1 tbs. vegetable oil
1 tbs. sugar
1½ tsp. salt
3-3¼ cups bread flour
2 tsp. rapid or quick yeast

Upon completion of the dough cycle, remove dough. Form rolls, place on a greased baking sheet, cover with a towel and let rise in a warm, draft-free location for 30 to 40 minutes. Bake in a preheated 400° oven for 12 to 15 minutes.

per 1 oz. 117 calories, 4 g protein, 21.5 g carbohydrate, 1.6 g fat, 0 mg cholesterol, 272 mg sodium

BANANA ORANGE NUT BREAD

Betty makes both breads on the dough cycle (put the first in the refrigerator after it is done and while the other one is in the machine.) Use fully ripe bananas for best moisture. Adjust moisture consistency if necessary. If your dough cycle has a raisin beep, add the nuts then. If not, add the nuts about 10 minutes after starting the machine. If desired, a glaze of confectioners' sugar, vanilla extract and milk may be drizzled on top while still warm.

DOUGH I

⅓ cup water
1 medium-sized fully ripe banana
1 tbs. vegetable oil
1 tbs. honey
1½ tsp. vanilla extract
½ tsp. salt

⅛ tsp. nutmeg, or to taste
⅔ cup oats (quick or old-fashioned)
1½ cups bread flour
1 tsp. vital gluten, optional
1 tsp. rapid or quick yeast
*½ cup chopped walnuts

DOUGH II

2/3 cup orange juice
1 tbs. vegetable oil
1 tbs. honey
1/2 tsp. salt
1/2 tsp. dried orange peel

1 cup oats (quick or old-fashioned)
1 1/4-1 1/2 cups bread flour
1/2 cup coconut flakes
1 tsp. rapid or quick yeast

After both doughs are finished, remove the first from the refrigerator and the second from the machine. Roll both into equal, thin rectangles, the width equal to the length of the loaf pan. Sprinkle one of the doughs with cinnamon and place the other dough on top. Roll the two rectangles together in a jelly roll fashion. Place in a medium to large loaf pan and let rise for about 30 minutes. Bake in a preheated 350° oven for 35 minutes or until golden brown.

per 1 oz.   *131 calories, 3.7 g protein, 20.3 g carbohydrate, 4.3 g fat, 0 mg cholesterol, 91 mg sodium*

SCALLION HERB ROLLS

MARY VOLLENDORF

Mary came up with these rolls for hamburgers or hot dogs. Toast rolls lightly on the grill to serve with meat. Milk gives a softer crumb, but either milk or water may be used. If using fresh, chopped basil, triple the amount. One teaspoon of liquid garlic or commercially prepared minced garlic may be used in place of the garlic clove. This may also be baked in either a 1½ lb. or 2 lb. machine. Makes 12.

1 cup milk or water
1 tbs. butter or margarine
1 egg
½-1 tsp. salt
1½ tsp. sugar

1 tsp. dried or liquid basil
1 garlic clove, minced
2 scallions, diced
3 cups bread flour
1½ tsp. rapid or quick yeast

After the dough cycle, remove dough from the machine and roll into a rectangle. Roll as a jelly roll from wide end to wide end, cut into 12 equal pieces and shape as desired. Place on a cornmeal-covered baking sheet, cover and allow to rise in a warm, draft-free location for 1 hour. Bake in a preheated 375° oven for 12 minutes.

---

per roll   121 calories, 4.3 g protein, 21.7 g carbohydrate, 1.9 g fat, 18 mg cholesterol, 197 mg sodium

DOUGHNUTS

PENNY LUCAS

Penny loves making these doughnuts, and her daughters (and my girls as well) have become addicted to them. Makes 12 to 15.

3/4 cup milk or water
2 eggs
4 tbs. butter
1 tsp. salt

1/3 cup sugar
3-3 1/4 cups all purpose flour
4 tsp. rapid or quick yeast

Upon completion of the dough cycle, punch down dough, remove it from the pan and let it rest for 10 minutes. On a lightly floured counter or board, roll dough out to about 1/2 inch thick and cut out rings with a floured doughnut cutter or with the open end of two glasses, one smaller than the other. Place on a greased baking sheet, cover and let rise for about an hour or until very light. Heat 4 cups of cooking oil in a deep fryer (375° if you have a temperature control). Add 2 or 3 doughnuts at a time and fry each side about 1 minute. Remove from oil and drain on paper towels. Glaze with powdered sugar mixed with a little water or milk, or dust with powdered sugar.

---

per 1/12 recipe   224 calories, 4.6 g protein, 29.8 g carbohydrate, 9.5 g fat, 46 mg cholesterol, 584 g sodium

SOURCES

Call for a catalog or price list.

FLOURS AND GRAINS

Arrowhead Mills, TX	806-364-0730	Gray's Grist Mill, RI	508-636-6075
Birket Mills, NY	315-536-3311	Great River Organic Milling, MN	507-457-0334
Bob's Red Mill		Kenyon's Corn Meal Co., RI	401-783-4054
Natural Foods, OR	503-654-3215	King Arthur's Flour, VT	800-827-6836
Brewster River Mill, VT	802-644-2987	Old Mill of Guilford, NC	919-643-4783
Brumwell Milling, IA	319-578-8106	Pamela's products, CA	415-952-4546
Country Harvest, UT	800-322-2245	Paul's Grains, IA	515-476-3373
Garden Spot Dist., PA	800-829-5100	Tadco/Niblack, NY	800-724-8883

SPICES

House of Spices, NY	718-476-1577	Sultan's Delight, NY	718-720-1557

For information about *The Bread Machine Newsletter* by Donna R. German, write to:

976 Houston Northcutt Blvd., Suite 3
Mt. Pleasant, SC 29464

Request a complimentary review copy. Send a stamped, self-addressed envelope.
You may also request additional information about bread machine makes and models; again, send a stamped, self-addressed envelope.

INDEX

SERVE CREATIVE, EASY, NUTRITIOUS MEALS WITH NITTY GRITTY® COOKBOOKS

Cappuccino/Espresso: The Book of
   Beverages
Worldwide Sourdoughs From Your
   Bread Machine
Indoor Grilling
Slow Cooking
The Best Pizza is Made at Home
The Well Dressed Potato
Convection Oven Cookery
The Steamer Cookbook
The Pasta Machine Cookbook
The Versatile Rice Cooker
The Dehydrator Cookbook
The Bread Machine Cookbook
The Bread Machine Cookbook II
The Bread Machine Cookbook III
The Bread Machine Cookbook IV
The Bread Machine Cookbook V

Recipes for the Pressure Cooker
The New Blender Book
The Sandwich Maker Cookbook
Waffles
The Coffee Book
The Juicer Book
The Juicer Book II
Bread Baking (traditional), revised
The Kid's Cookbook
No Salt, No Sugar, No Fat
   Cookbook, revised
Cooking for 1 or 2, revised
Quick and Easy Pasta Recipes,
   revised
15-Minute Meals for 1 or 2
The 9x13 Pan Cookbook
Extra-Special Crockery Pot Recipes

Chocolate Cherry Tortes and
   Other Lowfat Delights
Low Fat American Favorites
Now That's Italian!
Fabulous Fiber Cookery
Low Salt, Low Sugar, Low Fat
   Desserts
Healthy Cooking on the Run,
   revised
Healthy Snacks for Kids
Muffins, Nut Breads and More
The Wok
New Ways to Enjoy Chicken
Favorite Seafood Recipes
New International Fondue Cookbook
Favorite Cookie Recipes
Authentic Mexican Cooking
Fisherman's Wharf Cookbook

Write or call for our free catalog.
BRISTOL PUBLISHING ENTERPRISES, INC.
P.O. Box 1737, San Leandro, CA 94577
(800) 346-4889; in California (510) 895-4461